THE CENTO
A Collection of Collage Poems

edited by

Theresa Malphrus Welford

RED HEN PRESS | Pasadena, California

The Cento: A Collection of Collage Poems
Copyright © 2011 by Theresa Malphrus Welford

All rights reserved

No part of this book may be used or reproduced in any manner whatsoever without the prior written permission of both the publisher and the copyright owner.

Book layout by Andrew Mendez

ISBN: 978-1-59709-132-9 (tradepaper)
ISBN: 978-1-59709-452-8 (hardcover)

The Cento : A Collection of Collage Poems / Edited by Theresa Malphrus Welford. — 1st ed.
p. cm.
1. Found poetry, American. I. Welford, Theresa M.
PS593.F68C46 2011
811.008—dc23
2011020508

The Los Angeles County Arts Commission, the California Arts Council, the National Endowment for the Arts, and City of Los Angeles Department of Cultural Affairs partially support Red Hen Press.

First Edition

Published by Red Hen Press
www.redhen.org

THE CENTO

ACKNOWLEDGEMENTS

Bradford Allison, "Melancholy in the Pubic Domain": "She Dwelt Among the Untrodden Ways," William Wordsworth; "Across the Border," Sophie Jewett; "Lines Written in the Bay of Lerici," Percy Bysshe Shelley; "Ode to a Nightingale," John Keats; Canto 15, "The Rape of the Lock," Alexander Pope; "Sonnet XCIV," William Shakespeare; "She Walks in Beauty," Lord Byron; "Silent, Silent Night," William Blake; "To a Friend Whose Work Has Come to Nothing," William Butler Yeats; "A Better Resurrection," Christina Rossetti; "The Fire of Drift-Wood," Henry Wadsworth Longfellow; "Sohrab and Rustum," Matthew Arnold.

Nicole Andonov, "Morning with Pessoa": *Fernando Pessoa & Co.*, edited and translated from the Portuguese by Richard Zenith.

Jeanne Marie Beaumont, "Solace from Marianne": "What Are Years?"; "The Camperdown Elm"; "To a Giraffe"; "Sun"; "Charity Overcoming Envy"; "Silence"; "Tippo's Tiger"; "Like a Bulwark"; "Voracities and Verities Sometimes Are Interacting"; "Light Is Speech"; "Blue Bug"; "A Grave"; "Blessed Is the Man"; "Apparition of Splendor"; "A Carriage from Sweden"; "Nevertheless" (title + first line); "A Face"; "Tell Me, Tell Me"; "Rigorists"; "Bird-Witted"; "The Sycamore"; "The Steeple-Jack"; "Love in America?"; "I've Been Thinking..."; "The Mind Is an Enchanting Thing"; "Elephants"; "The Hero"; "Nine Nectarines and Other Porcelain" (later called "Nine Nectarines").

Lorna Blake, "Duke Ellington...": "The memory of things gone is important to a jazz musician," previously published April 29, 1999, "Duke Ellington's Centennial," *The New York Times*.

Linda Bosson, "Terminal Signs": First published in *RiverSedge*.

Marion Boyer, "How to Not Be Here When the Universe Dies": Lines from "How to Survive the End of the Universe" by Michio Kaku.

John Bradley, "There Is a World: Lee Harvey Oswald and the Seduction of History": Used with the permission of Don DeLillo.

Debbi Brody, "Santa Fe Soul Cento": Lines from members of writing group and from other writers: Debbi Brody: 1, 5, 10, 19, 26, 32, 36, 43, 48, 55, 61, 72, 82, 83, 100; Rachelle Woods: 2, 13, 14, 52, 69, 71, 79, 99; Maria Barcelona: 3, 49; Mary McGinnis: 4, 20, 27, 29, 38, 45, 54, 58, 62, 66, 74, 76, 80, 87, 97; Leslie Bentley: 6, 68, 93; Lauren Camp: 7, 25, 30, 44, 57, 64, 65; Michelle Holland: 8,9,21,22,92; Jane Lipman: 11,16,37,85,86; Leticia Lopez: 12, 23; Zoe Dwyer: 15,18,51,70,81,96; Apache Saying: 24; Lynn Holm: 28,33,60; Fred Mitchum: 31,35,56,77; Richard Wolfson: 34,46,59,63; Teresa Gallion: 39; Elizabeth Raby: 40; Dorothy Alexander: 41; Devey Napier: 42; Amelia Raymond: 47; Angela Janda: 50; Bobby Bermea: 53; Harry Garcia: 67; Gregory Corso: 73; Wendell Berry: 75; Rebecca Wolle: 78, 94; Ann Weisman: 84; Samara Grossman: 90; Marianne Moore: 91; Isabelle Allende: 95.

Kerri Buckley, "There Was Only the Sound of the Sea": Lines from Virginia Woolf.

Kerri Buckley, "Sea and Sky": Lines from Sylvia Plath.

Catherine Chandler-Oliveira, "I Had Some Things": Lines from Emily Dickinson.

Alex Cigale, "How the Animals Came Into This World": Lines from aboriginal myths, Kierkegaard, and others, plus some ad-libs.

Terese Coe, "Clooth-na-Bare": Previously published in *Candelabrum*. "September 1913"; "The

Sorrow of Love"; "No Second Troy"; "The Folly of Being Comforted"; "The Hosting of the Sidhe"; "The Land of Heart's Desire"; "Into the Twilight"; "The Old Men Admiring Themselves in the Water."

Terese Coe, "Trifles": Previously published in *The Shakespeare Newsletter*. *King Henry IV Part I*, III i; *Twelfth Night*, III iv; Sonnet 129; *Midsummer Night's Dream*, I i; Sonnet 97; Sonnet 86; Sonnet 119; Sonnet 97; *Venus and Adonis*; Sonnet 33; Sonnet 145; *Winter's Tale*, IV ii; Sonnet 129.

Allan Douglass Coleman, "Things to Remember About Shafting": *Stromberg's Steam User's Guide and Instructor* (St. Louis: Stromberg Publishing Co., 1894). Author unidentified.

Sharon Dolin, "Char'd Endings": Closing lines of poems by René Char.

Carol Dorf, "A Cento of Stolen Moments": Parra, Polya, Gardner, Ferlingetti, Jabes, Creeley, Levine, Piercy, Wilbur, Hall, Dove, and Hayden.

Carol Dorf, "You Had Meant to Catch It": Brecht, Borges, M. Moore, Krog, Chitwood, B. Smith, Grennen, C. Jones, Boruch, Finn, and Kinzie.

Edward Dougherty, "The Witness": Previously published in *Heartlands Today*. Sam Hamill, "The Necessity to Speak"; Anna Ahkmatova, *Selected Poetry*; Adolph Eichmann, *Eichmann Interrogated*; John Hersey, *Hiroshima*; Barry Lopez, *Arctic Dreams*; Rollo May, *The Courage to Create*; Rainer Maria Rilke, *Notebooks of Malte Laurids Brigge*; Walt Whitman, *Leaves of Grass*.

Lila Duckett, "A Villenella": Lines by Rita Dove.

Margarita Engle, "Fresh Produce Tabloid Headlines": Lines from grocery labels.

Margarita Engle, "He Who Cannot Run Flies": Lines from Cuban folklore.

Carmine Esposito, "Green is the Night and Out of Madness Woven": "Parts of a World," *The Collected Poems of Wallace Stevens* (New York: Knopf, 1972).

Carmine Esposito, "In the Center of Furies": Lines from Audre Lord.

Annie Finch, "Compassion for Scarpia": A demi-cento using lines from Tosca.

Richard Flynn, "Men of Our Time": Index, *Men of Our Time*. Moramarco, Fred, and Al Zolynas, editors. (Athens, GA: 1992).

Audrey Friedman, "Cento (Mark Doty, *Atlantis*)": First published in *Recursive Angel* http://www.recursiveangel.com, July 2001).

Diane Gersoni-Edelman, "Cento: Falls the Shadow": T.S. Eliot, "The Hollow Men"; Wallace Stevens, "The Ultimate Poem is Abstract"; Randall Jarrell, "The Emancipators"; Isaac Rosenberg, "Break of Day in the Trenches"; Conrad Aiken, IV from "Discordants"; Adrienne Rich, "Implosions"; Basil Bunting, "To Violet"; Allen Tate, "Sonnets of the Blood"; Thom Gunn, "High Fidelity"; Gwendolyn Brooks, "The Children of the Poor"; Robert Penn Warren, "Watershed"; Louis Untermeyer, "End of the Comedy"; Kathleen Raine, "The Instrument"; Randall Jarrell, "Aging"; James Merrill, "Mirror"; Peter De Vries, "Conscript." Except for "The Hollow Men," these poems appear in *The "Poetry" Anthology, 1912-2002* (Joseph Parisi and Stephen Young, eds.).

Dana Gioia, "A Brief History of Tobacco": Previously published in *Daily Horoscope* (Graywolf Press, 1986).

Dana Gioia, "Elegy with Surrealist Proverbs as Refrain": Previously published in *Interrogations at Noon* (Graywolf Press, 2001).

Anne Gorrick, "21st Century Girls: A Quarter-Cento": Reb Livingston; Laurel Snyder; Elizabeth Bradfield; Suzanne Burns; Amy King; Carly Saches; Marta Ferguson; Cami Park; Rebecca Loudon; Shanna Compton; Catherine Daly; Jill Alexander Essbaun; Molly Arden; Eden Osucha; Tatjana Lukic; Anne Boyer; Anne Gorrick; Jessica Grim; Harryette Mullen; Lauren Mullen; Leslie Scalapino; Maryrose Larkin; Mei-mei Berssenbrugge; Susan Howe; Mary Ruefle.

Michael Hanner, "On Finding a Book of Poems": First published in *Verseweavers*, 2006. Lines from *Moonmusic*, Toni Van Deusen.

Barbara Hantman, "Burns Festschrift": "Halloween"; "A Red, Red Rose"; "The Bonny Wee Thing"; "Afton Water"; "I Love My Jean"; "Green Grow the Rashes"; "Ae Fond Kiss"; "Corn Rigs"; "To a Mouse"; "Auld Lang Syne."

Barbara Hantman, "Gwendolyn Brooks: Medley of Wisdom": Brooks, *Blacks* (Third World Press, Chicago, Illinois, 2000).

Janis Butler Holm, "A Magazine of Bare, Naked Ladies": First published in *The Gay and Lesbian Review*, March-April 2005.

Janis Butler Holm, "Exercises in Subordination": Virginia Waddy, *Elements of Composition and Rhetoric with Copious Exercises in Both Criticism and Construction* (New York: American Book Company, 1889).

Mikhail Horowitz, "The Second Coming of the New Colossus": William Butler Yeats, "The Second Coming" (lines in Roman type); Emma Lazarus, "The New Colossus" (lines in italics).

Mikhail Horowitz, "Twenty Couplets": Anonymous; Blake; E. B. Browning; R. Browning; Burns; Byron; Coleridge; Corso; Crane; Cummings; de la Mare; Dickinson; Eliot; Fitzgerald; Frost; Ginsberg; Gray; Hopkins; Jarrell; Joyce; Keats; Kipling; Lindsay; Masters; McClure; Millay; Milton; Moore; Plath; Poe; Pound; Ransom; Sandburg; Shakespeare; Shelley; Stevens; Tennyson; Thomas; Whitman.

Troy Jollimore, "Rosencrantz and Guildenstern Are Dead, Ruined by Reading the Cantos of Ezra Pound: Or, Song of My Shelf": Previously published in *Exile: A Literary Quarterly*, and in *Tom Thomson in Purgatory* (Margie, Inc., 2006).

Jen Karetnick, "Centoum for Gin and Pilgrims": From signs around the Blackfriars Distillery in Plymouth, England

Diane Kendig, "On Frida Kahlo's *Diego on My Mind*": Previously published in *Poemeleon*.

Yala Korwin, "Let the Snake Wait": Lines in italics borrowed from "A Sort of a Song" by William Carlos Williams.

Karen Lewis, "Caught by the Light: A Cento": Lines from Margaret Atwood.

Mary Lyon, "That Would Be All of It": Lines from *New York Times* obituaries.

Martin McGowan, "Poetics": Housman; Eliot; Robinson; Fitzgerald; Lawrence; Tennyson; O. Sitwell; Pound; Moore; Hopkins; Sassoon; Kipling; Clough; Frost.

Martin McGowan, "Wet Bones": R. Browning; MacLeish; Donne; Ransom; Eliot; Hardy; Stevens; Pound; T. Gray; Jeffers; Crane; Herrick; Whitman; Swinburne; Lewis; Graves; Roethke; de la Mare; W. R. Rodgers; Flecker; Shakespeare.

Susan McLean, "Last Words: A Cento": D. G. Rossetti, "Retro Me, Sathana"; Roethke, "I Knew a Woman"; Yeats, "A Dialogue of Self and Soul"; Ralegh, "On the Life of Man"; Dunbar, "Ere Sleep Comes Down to Soothe the Weary Eyes"; Keats, "To Autumn"; Thomas, "Do Not Go Gentle into That Goodnight"; Bryant, "To Cole, the Painter, Departing for Europe"; Graves, "The Cool Web"; Frost, "The Wood-Pile"; Clare, "I Am"; de la Mare, "Goodbye."

Mary Moore, "Emily, Walking": Dickinson, poems numbered 520, 540, 542, 564, 416, 413, 327, 582, 1443, 1700, 1293, 1610, 1588, 1762, 87, 718.

Mary Moore, "View from a Hotel in Conshohocken, Pennsylvania": From *The Collected Poems of Wallace Stevens* (Vintage Paperback Edition, 1990).

Eileen Murphy, "when it rains (*Clouds* Cento #5)": *Clouds* translated by Ian Johnson.

Eileen Murphy, "Grimm Cento #2": From http://www.pitt.edu/~dash/folktexts.html

Deborah Nodler Rosen, "Dreaming Myself": C. Wright, "Looking Outside the Cabin Window, I Remember a Line by Li Po"; Brodsky, "On Love"; Kleinzahler, "Cat in Late Autumn"; Erdrich, "I Was Sleeping Where the Black Oaks Move"; Erdrich, "Indian Boarding School: The Runaways"; 6: C.Wright, "Reading Lao Tzu Again in the New Year"; Erdrich, "Time"; Walcott, "Sea Grapes"; Wislawa Szymborska, "Nothing Twice"; Sissman, "Homage to Clotho: A Hospital Suite"; Forche, "San Onofre, California"; N. Sachs, "And night step by step"; Dennis, "The Photograph"; Shihab Nye, "Advice"; Hirsch, "Under a Wild Green Fig Tree"; Kooser, "Walking on Tiptoe"; Hamilton Adair, "Having It All"; A. Carson, "The Glass Essay"; Kooser, "Surviving"; Li-Young Lee, "Furious Versions"; Santos, "Inspiration"; Santos, "The Perishing"; 23: Bishop, "At The Fishhouses"; 24 & 25: Hass, "Sunrise"; 26: Hirsch, "The Desire Manuscripts." (Note: All lines in "Dreaming Myself" have been quoted exactly from the sources listed, with the exception of line 21, in which the poet added "s" to the word "leave.")

Kathleen Ossip, "Ballade Confessionnelle: Plath and Sexton": Previously published in *The Search Engine* (APR/Copper Canyon, 2002).

Lynn Pattison, "Who But I": Lines from John Berryman's Sonnets To Chris, 1 & 2.

David Poston, "Cento, Selected Works": Previously published as "Cento, Titled," in *Main Street Rag* 6, 3 (Fall 2001): 52. Also included in a chapbook called *Postmodern Bourgeois Poetaster Blues*, winner of the 2007 North Carolina Writers' Network Randall Jarrell/Harperprints competition.

Steven Reigns, "To My Ex": Lines from songs written by Tori Amos.

Alicita Rodríguez, "Map of Bones": Sweeney, "The Summoning"; DeMorgan, "The Necklace of Princess Fiorimonde"; Seltzer, "Maumee River with Peaches"; Wilde, "The Selfish Giant"; Jimenez, "She Came, At First, Pure..."; Craik, "The Little Lame Prince and His Travelling Cloak"; Upton, "The Bull in the China Shop"; L. Johnson, "Babel"; Harms, "We Never Named Her Helen"; Zucker, "II. Soma, Germ-Plasm"; Heffland, "Photo: Man Holding Violin" by Jody Helfland; Thackeray, "The Rose and The Ring"; Haug, "Accumulation"; Parham, "Only This"; L. McGrath, "Marigolds"; Sterling, "Between For & From"; Macdonald, "The Golden Key"; Serpas, "The Discipline of Non-Fulfillment"; Ruskin, "The King of the Golden River"; Garner, "Elegy for Memory"; D. Shine, "Green Keys Nursery" by David Shine; S. Wade, "Little Body Songs"; Rash, "Luna" by Ron Rash; Kotaro, "Metropolis"; Panning, "Specs: My Life in Eyeglasses"; J. Cooper, "Transitory Endings" by Jack Cooper; Neruda, "Youth"; Agner, "Geese Speak"; W. Walker, *The Secret Service*.

Alicita Rodríguez, "Lion Tamarins": W. C. Williams, "Dawn"; H. D., "Eurydice"; Eliot, "The Love Song of J. Alfred Prufrock"; G. Harvey, "Temple of the Moon"; Stevens, "The Bird with the Coppery, Keen Claws"; Borich, "Serpents" by Borich; Rich, "Diving Into the Wreck"; Dickey, "The Heaven of Animals"; Rich, "Aunt Jennifer's Tigers"; L. Johnson, "Test Pattern with Red Flares"; Halloran, "The Shadow"; Fujiwara, "Dove Garden."

Lorraine Schein, "Word Balloon": Lines from Marvel comics.

Nancy Scott, "Now Is the Time": Previously published in *Against Forgetting*, edited by Carolyn Forché.

Wendy Shortridge, "Blood Bath": Lines from "Strange Meeting," Wilfred Owen.

Lucille Gang Shulklapper, "Fury": Bly, Clifton, Kunitz, Li-Young Lee, McCarriston, McPherson, Mura, Rich, Shihab Nye, Stafford, Stern, Tall Mountain, Zamora. Title and dedication from Lucille Clifton.

Torey Simons, "*Trichechus manatus latirostris*": Rogers, "Discovering Your Subject"; Wilbur, "The Pardon"; Clampitt, "Nothing Stays Put"; Dunn, "The Sacred"; R. Phillips, "The Stone Crab: A Love Poem"; Van Duyn, "Letters from a Father"; Snyder, "The Bath"; Carruth, "Woodsmoke at 70"; Geok-lin Lim, "Pantoun for Chinese Women"; S. Howe, "Closed Fist Withholding an Open Palm";

J. Carter, "Drawing the Antique" by Jared Carter; Ruark, "Lecturing My Daughters."

Jeanne Stauffer-Merle, "A Cento of Houses": John Ashbery: *Self Portrait in a Convex Mirror* and *Houseboat Days*; Baudelaire: *Les Fleurs du Mal*; Burkard: *The Fires They Kept* and *My Secret Boat*; Cummings: *XLI Poems*; Dolin: *Serious Pink*; M. Ford: *Soft Sift*; Sappho: *Collected Poems* (trans. Mary Barnard); Stevens: *The Palm at the End of the Mind*; Tranströmer: *The Half-Finished Heaven* (trans. Robert Bly); Valentine: *Home Deep Blue* and *Door in the Mountain*.

Juanita Torrence-Thompson, "A Cento of Lucy Angeleri's Poetry": From Angeleri's *Tidings II: 10 Aspects of Life in Poetry*. Used with permission.

Catherine Tufariello, "Spamtoum": First published in *Garbanzo!* http://www.garbanzo.us/index.htm.

Patricia Valdata, "Cento: The Waves Are Running in Verses": Bishop, "The Sandpiper," "At the Fishhouses," "The Armadillo," "Arrival at Santos," "Questions of Travel," "Invitation to Miss Marianne Moore," "While Someone Telephones," "Cape Breton," "Over 2,000 Illustrations and a Complete Concordance," "Florida," "Roosters," "Anaphora," "The Weed," "A Cold Spring," "Electrical Storm."

Irving Weiss, "Team Poem": Previously published in *Visual Voices* (Runaway Spoon Press, hand-printed by Mike Kaylor at the Literary House Press). Lines from Marvell, Dryden, Jonson, Pope, Wordsworth, Cowper, R. Browning, Drayton, G. Fletcher, Keats, Tennyson, Sackville, Randolph, Vaughan.

Theresa Malphrus Welford, "Fatima": Lines from *Arabian Jazz*, by Diana Abu-Jaber. Used with permission of the author.

Theresa Malphrus Welford, "Wide Like a River": E. B. Browning, cummings, Daub, Gioia, Gunn, E. Nelson, Neruda, Shihab Nye, Steele, and Wolverton.

Ingrid Wendt, "Paraphrase in Time of Thaw": Previously published in *Stafford's Road*, Thomas Ferte, ed. Monmouth, Oregon: Adrienne Lee Press, 1991.

Contributors included in the Acknowledgments provided information about their source materials. Since the authors of centos are not required to provide such information, others elected not to do so. If anything was omitted by accident, the editor humbly apologizes.

TABLE OF CONTENTS

DAVID LEHMAN
Introduction — 21

THERESA M. WELFORD
A Note from the Editor — 25

L. N. ALLEN
Robot Woman — 31

L. N. ALLEN
Ecclesiastes Redux — 32

BRADFORD ALLISON
Melancholy in the Public Domain — 34

NICOLE ANDONOV
Morning with Pessoa — 35

DODICI AZPADU
Holy Terror — 37

JEANNE MARIE BEAUMONT
Solace from Marianne — 40

F. J. BERGMANN
Cento Canto — 42

LORNA BLAKE
Duke Ellington — 47

LINDA BOSSON
Terminal Signs — 48

MARION BOYER
How To Not Be Here When The Universe Dies: A Cento-Sestina — 49

JOHN BRADLEY
There Is a World: Lee Harvey Oswald and the Seduction of History — 51

DEBBI BRODY
Santa Fe Soul Cento   54

BETH BROWNE
Junk Mail: A Found Poem   59

KERRI BUCKLEY
There Was Only the Sound of the Sea   60

KERRI BUCKLEY
Sea and Sky   62

NAN BYRNE
Giant   63

CATHERINE CHANDLER-OLIVEIRA
I had some things   64

CATHERINE CHANDLER-OLIVEIRA
The Bard   65

ALEX CIGALE
How the Animals Came Into this World   67

TERESE COE
Clooth-na-Bare   69

TERESE COE
Trifles   70

ALLAN DOUGLASS COLEMAN
Things to Remember about Shafting   71

PHILIP DACEY
Collage Sonnet: Thomas Eakins on Painting   73

PHILIP DACEY
Patchwork Sonnet of Friends' Complimentary Closes   74

MARTHA DEED
*Misunderestimated Will of Me in the Actual Unedited
Words of George W. Bush: A Fabulous Year
for Laura and Me (December 2011)*   75

MARTHA DEED
River Road Cento: a Sevening   77

SHARON DOLIN
Char'd Endings   78

CAROL DORF
A Cento of Stolen Moments   79

CAROL DORF
You Had Meant to Catch It   80

EDWARD DOUGHERTY
The Witness   81

LILA W. DUCKETT
A Villanella   85

ELLEN ELDER
My Mother's Ashes   86

MARGARITA ENGLE
He Who Cannot Run Flies   88

MARGARITA ENGLE
Fresh Produce Tabloid Headlines   89

CARMINE ESPOSITO
In the Center of Furies   90

CARMINE ESPOSITO
Green Is the Night and Out of Madness Woven   91

MARGARET FIELAND
    Twelve Drummers Drumming: A Haiku Sequence   94

ANNIE FINCH
    Compassion for Scarpia   95

SUSAN FIRER
    Call Me Pier   98

RICHARD FLYNN
    Men of Our Time   99

JACK FOLEY
    Valentine's Day Cento (Chaucer/Milton/Pope/Byron/Shelley/
    Baudelaire/Joyce): The Radio Changes Poet Channels   101

AUDREY FRIEDMAN
    Cento (Mark Doty, Atlantis)   103

KATE GALE
    Did you ever dance with the devil in the pale moonlight?   105

DIANE GERSONI-EDELMAN
    Cento: Falls the Shadow   106

DANA GIOIA
    A Short History of Tobacco   107

DANA GIOIA
    Elegy with Surrealist Proverbs as Refrain   109

ANNE GORRICK
    21st Century Girls: A Quarter-Cento   111

KATE GREENSTREET
    eclipsed   112

KATE GREENSTREET
 He learns he was given a secret name   114

R. S. GWYNN
 Approaching a Significant Birthday, He Peruses
 The Norton Anthology of Poetry   115

KIMBERLY HAMILTON
 Land of the Fairy Chimneys   117

MARYANNE HANNAN
 An American Cento   118

MICHAEL HANNER
 On Finding a Book of Poems   120

BARBARA HANTMAN
 Burns Festschrift   122

BARBARA HANTMAN
 Gwendolyn Brooks: Medley of Wisdom   123

H. L. HIX
 Letter to Dana Gioia   125

H. L. HIX
 Letter to Philip Brady   128

JANIS BUTLER HOLM
 A Magazine of Bare, Naked Ladies   130

JANIS BUTLER HOLM
 Exercises in Subordination   131

MIKHAIL HOROWITZ
 The Second Coming of the New Colossus   133

MIKHAIL HOROWITZ
   Twenty Couplets   134

DARREN JACKSON
   At the Hour of Love and Blue Eye Lids   138

TROY JOLLIMORE
   Rosencrantz and Guildenstern Are Dead,
       Ruined by Reading the Cantos *of Ezra Pound*   143

GENEVIEVE KAPLAN
   133   148

GENEVIEVE KAPLAN
   166   149

JEN KARETNICK
   Centoum for Gin and Pilgrims   150

DIANE KENDIG
   On Frida Kahlo's Diego on My Mind   151

TRACEY KNAPP
   Blonde   152

PHYLLIS KOESTENBAUM
   What Would I Do Without This
       World Faceless Incurious: A Cento   153

YALA KORWIN
   Let the Snake Wait   155

JANE K. KRETSCHMANN
   Volatile Territories   156

DAVID LEHMAN
   December 14   157

DAVID LEHMAN
    Touchstones   158

KAREN LEWIS
    Caught by the Light: A Cento   160

MARY LYON
    That Would Be All of It   163

MIKE MAGGIO
    A Muscle Disease, a Stream of Clear, Pure Water All Dried Up   164

MARTIN McGOWAN
    Poetics   167

MARTIN McGOWAN
    Wet Bones   168

SUSAN McLEAN
    Last Words: A Cento   170

MARY MOORE
    Emily, Walking   171

MARY MOORE
    View from a Hotel in Conshohocken, Pennsylvania   172

WILDA MORRIS
    Astrophel and Stella   173

CHRISTOPHER MULROONEY
    cento   174

EILEEN MURPHY
    when it rains (Clouds Cento #5)   175

EILEEN MURPHY
    Grimm Cento #2   176

ERIC NELSON
Dickinson's Island   178

DEBORAH NODLER ROSEN
Dreaming Myself   179

GEORGE NORTHRUP
Nos Morituri Te Salutamus   181

KATHLEEN OSSIP
Ballade Confessionnelle: Plath and Sexton   182

LYNNE PATTISON
Who But I   184

DAVID POSTON
Cento, Selected Works   186

MARJORIE POWER
Fall Runway Report   189

MARJORIE POWER
Wander Woman   190

ANN PRIVATEER
Dove Promises   191

ANN PRIVATEER
Untitled   192

BURT RASHBAUM
Stolen Wind Poem   193

STEVEN REIGNS
To My Ex   195

ALICITA RODRÍGUEZ
Map of Bones   196

ALICITA RODRÍGUEZ
Lion Tamarins — 198

LORRAINE SCHEIN
World Balloon — 199

NANCY SCOTT
Now Is the Time — 200

WENDY SHORTRIDGE
Blood Bath — 202

LUCILLE GANG SHULKLAPPER
Fury — 204

MARTHA SILANO
New Mother Cento — 205

TOREY SIMONS
Trichechus manatus latirostris — 206

DANNY SKLAR
Never Start a Sentence with There — 207

JEANNE STAUFFER-MERLE
A Cento of Houses — 209

BARBARA TAYLOR
On *Silk and Soul* — 211

BARBARA TAYLOR
Things to Remember — 213

JUANITA TORRENCE-THOMPSON
A Cento of Lucy Angeleri's Poetry — 214

CATHERINE TUFARIELLO
Spamtoum   215

HELEN TZAGOLOFF
Cento   217

HELEN TZAGOLOFF
Midnight   218

PATRICIA VALDATA
Cento: The Waves Are Running in Verses   219

SUSAN VOLCHOK
Standing Here/Now   220

IRVING WEISS
Team Poem   223

THERESA MALPHRUS WELFORD
Fatima   224

THERESA MALPHRUS WELFORD
Like a Wide River   226

INGRID WENDT
Paraphrase in Time of Thaw   228

INTRODUCTION

These Fragments I Have Shored (first published in the *New York Times*, 2 April 2006)
     —David Lehman

A cento is a collage-poem composed of lines lifted from other sources—often, though not always, from great poets of the past. In Latin the word *cento* means "patchwork," and the verse form resembles a quilt of discrete lines stitched together to make a whole. The word *cento* is also Italian for "one hundred," and some mosaic poems consist of exactly 100 lines culled by one poet from the work of another to pay tribute to him or her. The ancient Greeks assembled centos in homage to Homer, the Romans in homage to Virgil.

Ever since T. S. Eliot raided Elizabethan drama and 17th-century poetry for "The Waste Land," the collage has held a strong attraction for modern poets. The cento as contemporary poets practice it is a specialized form of the collage: an anthology poem from diverse sources. John Ashbery did one called "To a Waterfowl" in 1961, and it is so good I was tempted to include it in the new edition of *The Oxford Book of American Poetry*. I still remember one couplet by heart: "Calm was the day and through the trembling air, / Coffee and oranges in a sunny chair." The first line is by Edmund Spenser, the second by Wallace Stevens, and the combined effect is the magic of Ashbery.

Writing a cento may be a kind of extension of the act of reading, a way to prolong the pleasure. What makes the cento so appealing a poetic form—and one with increasing popularity—is the opportunity to revel in quotations and yoke them strategically for a variety of effects beginning with surprise and humor and ending sometimes in clarity and vision. After editing this new anthology, I felt inevitably drawn to the idea of forging a cento from its pages, in honor of the poets and as a souvenir of the experience of working on the project. Here it is:

THE OXFORD CENTO

If the sun shines but approximately[1]
Only where love and need are one,[2]
Who in this Bowling Alley bowld the Sun?[3]
Of whom shall we speak? For every day they die[4]
Younger than their kids—jeans, ski-pants, sneakers.[5]
And the stars never rise but I see the bright eyes[6]
Waking far apart on the bed, the two of them.[7]
And so it was I entered the broken world.[8]
Good morning, Daddy![9]
Every woman adores a Fascist,[10]
Doing a man's work, though a child at heart.[11]
When I am slitting a fish's head,[12]
Would he like it if I told him?[13]
Odd that a thing is most itself when likened,[14]
Everything only connected by "and" and "and."[15]
There are no flowers in Hell.[16]

---

1   Laura Riding, "'The World and I."
2   Robert Frost, "Two Tramps in Mud Time."
3   Edward Taylor, "The Preface" to "God's Determinations Touching His Elect."
4   W. H. Auden, "In Memory of Sigmund Freud."
5   James Merrill, "Self-Portrait in Tyvek™ Windbreaker."
6   Edgar Allan Poe, "Annabel Lee."
7   John Ashbery, "Decoy."
8   Hart Crane, "The Broken Tower."
9   Langston Hughes, "Good Morning" from "Montage of a Dream Deferred."
10   Sylvia Plath, "Daddy."
11   Robert Frost, "'Out, Out—.'"
12   Elinore Wylie, "The Puritan's Ballad."
13   Gertrude Stein, "If I Told Him: A Completed Portrait of Picasso."
14   Richard Wilbur, "Lying."
15   Elizabeth Bishop, "Over 2,000 Illustrations and a Complete Concordance."
16   H. Phelps Putnam, "Bill Gets Burned."

Give all to love,[17]
A burnt match skating in a urinal[18]
That never lost a vote (O Adlai mine).[19]
What you get married for if you don't want children?[20]
And because it is my heart,[21]
Above, below, around, and in my heart,[22]
Blessed be God! For he created Death![23]
And rock-grained, rack-ruined battlements.[24]
One's sex asserts itself. Desire[25]
And that White Sustenance—[26]
Despair[27]—in a Sahara of snow,[28]
As a sort of mournful cosmic last resort.[29]
Meanwhile, the men, with vestiges of pomp,[30]
Weep for what little things could make them glad.[31]
We hurt each other as the bridegroom and the bride hurt each other.[32]
And I wish I did not feel like your mother.[33]

17	Ralph Waldo Emerson, "Give All to Love."
18	Hart Crane, "The Tunnel."
19	John Berryman, "Dream Song No. 23."
20	T. S. Eliot, "The Waste Land."
21	Stephen Crane, "In the Desert."
22	Conrad Aiken, from "Preludes."
23	Henry Wadsworth Longfellow, "The Jewish Cemetery at Newport."
24	Jean Garrigue, "Song in Sligo."
25	Herman Melville, "After the Pleasure Party."
26	Emily Dickinson, "I Cannot Live With You."
27	Emily Dickinson, "I Cannot Live With You."
28	Robert Lowell, "For the Union Dead."
29	Anthony Hecht, "The Dover Bitch."
30	Jean Toomer, "Georgia Dusk."
31	Robert Frost, "Directive."
32	Walt Whitman, "Song of Myself."
33	Edna St. Vincent Millay, "Rendezvous."

Thou ill-formed offspring of my feeble brain,[34]
There is nothing lowly in the universe.[35]
I have known the inexorable sadness of pencils,[36]
The sea in a chasm, struggling to be[37]
Unchanging, yet so like our perishing earth,[38]
On this green bank, by this soft stream,[39]
Where strangers would have shut the many doors,[40]
Except the one she sang and, singing, made.[41]
Heard on the street, seen in a dream, heard in the park, seen by the light of day,[42]
What is yours is mine my father.[43]
What more is there to do, except stay? And that we cannot do.[44]
And this is not as good a poem as The Circus[45]
Especially the lines that are spoken in the voice of the mouse.[46]
He opened the car door and looked back[47]
And clapped his hands and shouted to the birds.[48]
And that was the whole show.[49]

---

34   Anne Bradstreet, "The Author to Her Book."
35   A. R. Ammons, "Still."
36   Theodore Roethke, "Dolor."
37   Marianne Moore, "What Are Years?"
38   Wallace Stevens, "Sunday Morning."
39   Ralph Waldo Emerson, "Concord Hymn."
40   Edwin Arlington Robinson, "Mr. Flood's Party."
41   Wallace Stevens, "The Idea of Order at Key West."
42   Kenneth Fearing, "Green Light."
43   Walt Whitman, "As I Ebb'd With the Ocean of Life."
44   John Ashbery, "The Instruction Manual."
45   Kenneth Koch, "The Circus (1975)."
46   Billy Collins, "Workshop."
47   Galway Kinnell, "Hitchhiker."
48   Robert Pinsky, "From the Childhood of Jesus."
49   Charles Simic, "Country Fair."

A NOTE FROM THE EDITOR

As I was putting this collection together, one of the contributors, Allan Douglass Coleman, brought up several thought-provoking ideas. "Is 'cento' just another word for found poem," he asked, "an attempt to gussy up that concept (as *giclée* is used to gussy up ink-jet prints in the fine-art field) and perhaps give it a history that goes back further than the early twentieth century?" He goes on to explain his reasoning:

> As this may suggest (and as my poems probably don't), I'm something of a formalist, something of a traditionalist, and even something of a conservative. By this I mean that I think forms in art arise for a purpose, and that their transformation, violation, or abandonment should happen purposefully and consciously. I don't want to be the poetry equivalent of Moliere's bourgeois gentleman, proudly discovering that I've been generating centos all my life.

Coleman explains further:

> I suppose my underlying query—and perhaps my suggestion—is that an anthology such as you propose, which as the first of its kind will stand for some time as definitive, requires a more precise and rigorous definition of the form than you provide in your guidelines. . . .

First of its kind? Perhaps so. *Definitive?* I'm not so sure. This collection may *help* to define the term "cento," but my main goal is, simply, to present an intriguing array of poems in a form that I've grown to love. Also, to be honest, I simply started using the term "cento," then got in the habit. Other terms, such as "collage poems," "patchwork poems," and "mosaics," are equally appealing to me.

The original rules for the "cento" form *were* quite strict. However, as David Lehman suggests in his introduction, the rules and the definition have evolved over the years.

In selecting the poems for this collection, I have used the definition Lehman gives in his opening paragraph:

> A cento is a collage-poem composed of lines lifted from other sources—often, though not always, from great poets of the past. In Latin the word *cento* means "patchwork," and the verse form resembles a quilt of discrete lines stitched together to make a whole.

And, about that "bourgeois gentleman" in Moliere . . . I don't mind confessing that, in this case, I'm the female version of that fellow, who was tickled to learn that he'd been using prose his whole life. I wrote a cento before I'd even heard of the form. In the late 1990s, I sent Dana Gioia a copy of a poem that I'd composed using mix-and-match snippets from Emily Dickinson. He very kindly wrote back and congratulated me on my cento. *Cento?* I had to look up the term in my dictionary of poetry. From that day on, I began studying the form, and I became hooked. Similarly, several contributors to this book told me that they'd also been interested in this type of poem for a long time but hadn't known what to call it. Should we have known sooner? Well, yes. Knowledge is, after all, a good thing. But learning is exciting whenever it takes place, whether it happens in the "right" order or not.

I first encountered a collage poem when I was about ten years old, reading my Companion Library edition of *Huckleberry Finn* (which has *Tom Sawyer* on the flip side). At the time, I didn't understand what I was seeing, but the encounter has stayed with me nevertheless. Huck and Jim run into a pair of con artists who claim to be a "duke" and a "dauphin" in exile. In the passage below, Huck describes the fake duke's preparations to deliver his soliloquy:

> So he went to marching up and down, thinking, and frowning horrible every now and then; then he would hoist up his eyebrows; next he would squeeze his hand on his forehead and stagger back and kind of moan; next he would sigh, and next he'd let on to drop a tear . . . Then he strikes a most noble attitude, with one leg shoved forwards, and his arms stretched away up, and his head tilted

back, looking up at the sky; and then he begins to rip and rave and grit his teeth; and after that, all through his speech, he howled, and spread around, and swelled up his chest, and just knocked the spots out of any acting ever *I* see before.

I love to envision Samuel Clemens in his study, creating a soliloquy that's exactly right for this character, gleefully patching together snippets of various sizes, shapes, and colors from *Hamlet* and *Macbeth* and adding to the hilarity by stitching in a few pieces that are misshapen or mismatched.

I'll quit talking about it so that I can show it to you. At long last, here's Huck Finn's rendition of the fake duke's rendition of Hamlet's soliloquy:

> To be, or not to be, that is the bare bodkin
> That makes calamity of so long life;
> For who would fardels bear, till Birnam Wood do come to Dunsinane,
> But that the fear of something after death
> Murders the innocent sleep,
> Great nature's second course,
> And makes us rather sling the arrows of outrageous fortune
> Than fly to others that we know not of.
> There's the respect must give us pause:
> Wake Duncan with thy knocking! I would thou couldst;
> For who would bear the whips and scorns of time,
> The oppressor's wrong, the proud man's contumely,
> The law's delay, and the quietus which his pangs might take,
> In the dead waste and muddle of the night, when churchyards yawn
> In customary suits of solemn black,
> But that the undiscovered country from whose bourne no traveler returns,
> Breathes forth contagion on the world,
> And thus the native hue of resolution, like the poor cat i' the adage,
> Is sickled o'er with care,
> And all the clouds that lowered o'er our housetops,

With this regard their currents turn awry,
And lose the name of action.
'Tis a consummation devoutly to be wished. But soft: you, the fair Ophelia:
Ope not thy ponderous and marble jaws,
But get thee to a nunnery—go!

Well. That just knocks the spots out of any soliloquy ever *I* see before.

Anyway, I, too, value traditional poetic forms, but I'm very much a fan of doing what Ezra Pound suggested in the early 1900s: "Make it new!" Take what's old and shake it up, breathe new life into it. The cento form does exactly that. It can also take what's new and make it even newer and fresher. It's an active—and exhilarating—way of reading, interpreting, and appreciating existing works, with the added bonus of creating new ones.

As David Lehman suggests, writing a cento can be an "extension of the act of reading," a "way to prolong the pleasure," and an "opportunity to revel in quotations and yoke them strategically." How right he is. This past spring, after reading *Life of Pi*, by Yann Martel, I couldn't resist:

> Tell Me Stories
>
> —from *Life of Pi*
>
> Tell me stories:
> rich, noisy, functioning madness,
> the selective transforming of reality,
> hard to believe, elusive, irrational,
> grand, simple and gripping.
> The word, the word:
> ruddy with life.
> Bright, loud, swift as a swallow,

urgent as an ambulance.
A crescendo, a rousing rendition,
the star of the show,
wild and unpredictable.
Authenticity, crackling with tension,
unbelievable as the moon catching fire.
All the lands and seas of the earth
and the life in them,
hard, firm, certain land.
The road, the sea,
the trees, the air, the sun.
Chocolate. Bananas.
Tigers or orang-utans, hyenas or zebras,
meerkats or mongooses,
giraffes or hippopotamuses.
Trucks and buses and cars
and bicycles and pedestrians.
Shine and power and might,
outrage and pity and grief and bravery,
selfishness, anger, ruthlessness,
indignation and disgust.
Nightmares tinged with love,
the strangeness of the human heart.
Fear and sadness, awe and envy,
love and admiration and fear,
all ideas and all emotions,
all pity and all hope,
all the winds, all the nights
and all the moons.
Moments of wonder,
thoughts that span the universe.
What art, what might:

utter lucidity, the light of words,
lightning striking the sea.
A mystery, a thrilling show,
an epic simplicity,
utterly, majestically silent,
powerful, scary, wild and triumphant,
subject to explosions,
vast and fantastic,
rich as gold or honey.
Truth be told, greater truth,
strange, sometimes inexplicable.
Beyond understanding,
beyond description,
beyond approach.
The unknown, the twisting of it
to bring out its essence:
manifold expressions of life.

And, now, I'll step aside and let the poems in this collection—centos, mosaics, collage poems, patchwork poems—speak for themselves.

L. N. ALLEN

Robot Woman

—As found in Sunday's Ads

It cleans. It softens. What's not to love?
New Look! Same Great Taste!
Baggy eyes gone!
Baked not Fried.
Looks great! Light weight! Top rate!
Superior Sliding + Refreshing Clean.
Udderly natural.
Savor the Flaky Layers!
Hot and Fresh in Minutes!
Personalized to bring you a world of good fortune.
Can you change your destiny before noon?
It's about trust.
Try me and save $1.00.
Ready in no time. Because that's how much you have.

L. N. ALLEN

Ecclesiastes Redux

It's Howdy Doody time
apple blossom time
In the Good Old Summertime
all the time in the world

Kiss me once, and kiss me twice, and kiss me once again,
It's been a long, long time
Younger than springtime, are you
My Time is Your Time
Day time, night time, any old time
we're wonderful, 1 x 1

Time On My Hands
I'll have the time of my life
Till the end of time
Two Tramps in Mud Time
Keeping time, time, time in a sort of runic rhyme

Time marches on
time is money
spend time, waste time, spare time
lose time, keep time, save time
playing for time

The Last Time I Saw Paris
It was the best of times, it was the worst of times
Of Time and the River

end time
Time after time, I tell myself that I'm
behind the times, old as time, out of time, Father Time
Time and tide wait for no man
Time to put away childish things
time to refrain from embracing
Time to go, let's have one cigarette
time to place your bets
HURRY UP IT'S TIME

BRADFORD ALLISON

Melancholy in the Public Domain

She dwelt among the untrodden ways
Where all the trees bear golden flowers,

She left me at the silent time
My heart aches, and a drowsy numbness pains

She said: the pitying audience melt in tears,
They that have power to hurt and will do none,

She walks in beauty, like the night
Silent, silent night

Now all the truth is out,
I have no wit, no words, no tears;

We sat within the farm-house old,
AND the first grey of morning fill'd the east.

NICOLE ANDONOV

Morning with Pessoa

This morning I went out very early,
Because I woke up even earlier
And had nothing I wanted to do.

There is in each thing an animating essence.
In plants it's a tiny nymph that exists on the outside.
In man it's the soul that lives with him and is him.
And I, who have eyes that are only for seeing,
See an absence in all things.

The child knows how it is that things exist.
He knows existence exists and cannot be explained,
And he knows that to exist is to occupy a point.
What he doesn't know is that thought is not a point.

Today I wish I could think of Spring as a person.
But Spring isn't even a thing:
Nothing returns, nothing repeats.
Not even the flowers or green leaves return.
There are new flowers, new green leaves.
For me this sun,
these meadows, these flowers are enough.
But if they weren't enough,
What I would want is a sun more sun than the sun,
Meadows more meadows than these meadows,

Flowers more flowers than these flowers—
Everything more than what it is in the same way,
the same manner.

I lifted my right hand to wave at the sun,
I was glad I could still see it.

DODICI AZPADU

Holy Terror

The perfect artist / passes through / afflictions
in order to give / universes, races, and nations
geometry, physics, and mathematics.
The faithful / flow / pure in
all their milk.

Safe from being belittled / from incongruity
at all times and places / spiritual creations
repair one's broken hopes. / Fame and fortune
ground / each thing / lacking
one who can enforce.

Servants know / the highest level / contains
the good and the bad / without
the beloved and the hated /dangers of
loss and perdition / bearing no resemblance to
the woolen cloak.

When we find / the throne and the canopy
in accordance with / doubt and sadness
hidden in everything /watched and recorded,
everyone will / given the power
make gods out of their / swords.

Nothing escapes / hearts / destined to go
to the intermediary / the unforgivable sin:
associating equals with / garbage and thorns
to bear / powerful / malingerers.

On the day of the conquest
between his shoulder blades
the clement one / cancels man's distortions
from the city of Mecca to Jerusalem.
Bliss and comfort / pleasure and paradise
most generous / glory of the Arabs / who believe.
Superior / knight / guide to good deeds
curer of sick hearts / true counselor
who has no teacher / the helmet of the holy
whose fire burns / the doors of hell and
brings dead hearts to life.

The unlettered one / constantly sincere
toward those who tyrannize / our prayers
witness / acts in / answer to / the fragrant
distinguisher / torch.

Punish the sins of the believers
upon the universe / brains boiling in
darkness / the messengers / promised
the dirt of the world / desires of the flesh
as a mercy / on the ground.

In prostration / when the moon is full
pious and chaste / jinn and angels
gather around / the believers.
The last one who follows and contains all
will not be able to / cleanse us of
revenge against injustice.

JEANNE MARIE BEAUMONT

Solace from Marianne

What is our innocence,
I think, in connection with this weeping elm,

If it is unpermissible, in fact fatal
"No man may him hyde . . ."

Have you time for a story
My father used to say,

The tiger was his prototype.
Affirmed. Pent by power that holds it fast

I don't like diamonds;
One can say more of sunlight

In this camera shot,
Man looking into the sea,

Blessed is the man who does not sit in the seat of the scoffer—
Partaking of the miraculous

They say there is a sweeter air
Nevertheless you've seen a strawberry

I am not treacherous, callous, jealous, superstitious,
where might there be a refuge for me

We saw reindeer
With innocent wide penguin eyes, three

Against a gun-metal sky
Dürer would have seen a reason for living

Whatever it is, it's a passion—
Make a fuss

The mind is an enchanting thing
Uplifted and waved till immobilized

Where there is personal liking we go.
Arranged by two's as peaches are.

F. J. BERGMANN

Cento Canto

It came upon a midnight clear
Its fleece was white as snow
Did you ever see such a sight in your life?
No, my love, no

Are you sad? Are you cross? Are you gathering moss?
I'll find a reason to believe that it's all true
Don't bogart that joint, my friend
Rebel without a clue

We don't need no education
We three kings of Orient are
I can't get no satisfaction
How I wonder what you are

This land is your land; this land is my land
I wanna hold your hand
All in the fall, in the fall of the year
Walking in a winter wonderland

The bear went over the mountain
Where the deer and the antelope play
Her legs went on forever
Singing polly-wolly-doodle all the day

Way down upon the Swanee River
Deep and crisp and even
The sun so hot I froze to death
So I dub thee Unforgiven

Suicide is painless
With an illegal smile
Wild, wild horses
Riding many a mile

I'll never be your beast of burden
I, said the donkey, shaggy and brown
And you won't need no camel
'Cause it's such a long way down

I spied a young cowboy all wrapped in white linen
How still we see thee lie
The scaffold is high, eternity near
To take you to his mansion in the sky

Riders on the storm
Where the skies are blue
All the winds are laughing
'Cause you're unforgiven, too

It's the end of the world as we know it
I've been Rolling Stoned and Beatled till I'm blind
Don't go out tonight; it's bound to take your life
And there are no diamonds in the mine

You're blinded by rainbows
The mist like an angel's gown
Hey, you; don't tell me there's no hope at all
Santa Claus is coming to town

Oh, show me the way to the next whiskey bar
And the fool on the hill
O when the saints come marching in
Show me the way to Bar & Grill

Faster horses, younger women
And your horse naturally won
Some are born to a sweet delight
That ain't the way to have fun, son

I was betrayed by Flora
The pain it was sharp as a knife
Well, sharpen it, dear Henry, dear Henry, dear Henry
Has anybody seen my life?

You gotta keep 'em separated
Let the bodies hit the floor
And never mind that noise you heard
In 1984

Lucy in the sky with diamonds
Yesterday don't matter when it's gone
Please allow me to introduce myself
Devil with a blue dress on

Ninety-nine bottles of beer on the wall
One more joint to kill the pain
One more silver dollar
And I hoist my axe again

If I could keep time in a bottle
Have some Madeira, my dear
If I had a rocket launcher
Oh I wish that you were here

Oh my darling, oh my darling
When I squeeze you, you make noise
Your brother's gonna kill me and he's six feet ten
And I don't have a choice

He's dressed in a silver-sparked glittering gown
Keep me searching for a heart of gold
Hey babe, take a walk on the wild side
What a drag it is getting old

These boots were made for walking
Look what those five feet can do
Stop! In the name of love!
Ah-roooooo

Swing low, sweet chariot
Bring me my arrows of desire
Merrily, merrily, merrily, merrily
Try to set the night on fire

By the waters of Babylon
It's a hard rain's gonna fall
We all live in a yellow submarine
And drown in alcohol

Maybe in another life
Oh bring back my bonnie to me
Yes, we have no bananas
I have tried in my way to be free

LORNA BLAKE

Duke Ellington

once said, "The memory of things gone is important

 In a Sentimental Mood, Mood Indigo,

to a jazz musician." Jazz is the memory of things—

 Perdido, Flamingo. Lotus Blossom, Solitude,

things gone. The memory of the musician is important;

 Prelude to a Kiss, Sophisticated Lady, Satin Doll,

the jazz musician is gone and so many things are gone.

 I Got It Bad and That Ain't Good, All Too Soon,

Jazz is important to the memory of things gone.

 Moon Mist, Day Dream, Drawing Room Blues,

What is gone? The music of things, the memories . . .

 Blue Serge, Lover Man, Caravan, Chelsea Bridge,

The memory of things gone is important to a jazz musician.

 Jump for Joy, Come Sunday, Take the "A" Train.

LINDA BOSSON

Terminal Signs

—Grand Central Terminal, New York

Arrivals. Departures. Men. Women.
Do not rest
umbrellas on escalator steps.
Check your bags here.
Trash. Bottles and Cans.
Lost and Found. Men. Women.
Caution! Achtung! Cuidado!
Exit to Street.
No person shall spit on or upon
any terminal, station or train.
Do not rest
umbrellas on escalator steps.
Achtung! Cuidado!
Danger. No Clearance.
Restrooms.
Do not rest umbrellas.
Do not rest.
Do not.
Information. Trash. Tickets. Danger.
No person shall spit
on or upon.
No person shall.
No person. No.
Arrivals. Departures. Bottles. Cans.
Men. Women. Lost. Found.

MARION BOYER

How To Not Be Here When The Universe Dies: A Cento-Sestina

We are familiar with calamities: pestilences, the black
power of volcanoes, a nuclear bomb, civilizations
foamy and unstable, a frothing consumption of energy
and plenty of other problems beyond the expanding hole
in the weather. Now drifting in is intelligence
of the Big Freeze, absolute zero, end of the universe.

Today, physicists confirmed the universe
is out of control and it has them scrambling to their black
boards huddling around the flickering embers of intelligence
creating a survival guide. An advanced civilization
might try an escape plan, a suitable exit or wormhole
that connects here to there. Fleeing requires energy

(the total output of a galaxy); however, energy
should weigh less than nothing, and stacked on our universe
may be a neighboring one. It is possible. Black holes
are plentiful and might do the trick. To journey through a black
hole safely . . . here a problem arises. For a civilization
the trip would be fatal. So much for intelligence.

Why not start now, do some trial runs? Obviously, our intelligence
is limited. Hope waves from extremely far away. Deriving our energy
from dead plants, we qualify as a "Type 0" civilization.
A Type III could control the galaxy and leave this universe.
Nothing in physics forbids the scientist form a black
hole, create Alice's looking glass and fall up the hole.

How? First, gather swirling neutron stars to form a black hole.
Stir gently! This requires Type III intelligence.
One big bang and an explosion kicks everything into black
particles about the size of Manhattan. Messy. Negative energy.
Space littered with dead stars. Another option: Make a universe!
We'll need plenty of empty space and a Type III civilization.

A baby universe might equal only a few ounces. For any civilization,
acquiring a few ounces of matter is easy. Two: Acquiring a wormhole.
Three: Build a cosmic atom smasher and see what happens. If our universe
is closed, which it isn't, a laser implosion should open it. Intelligence
assumes millions of lasers, each powered by nuclear energy
firing before the stars exhaust, end of film, cut to black.

How to survive the end of the universe? Theoretically, civilization
has billions of years to perfect intelligence, probe a black
hole, harness energy. No time like the present to start planning!

JOHN BRADLEY

There Is a World: Lee Harvey Oswald and the Seduction of History

—Three villanelles

1.
Stalin's name was Dzhugashvili.
How many people know a killdeer is a bird?
There is a world inside the world.

The boy is in the yellow house.
When I read Hemingway, I get hungry.
Stalin's name was Dzhugashvili.

The id is hell. Even now
Crosshairs are centered on the back of your neck.
There is a world inside the world.

Every room has a music of its own.
Attention, Eduardo, the moon is red.
Stalin's name was Dzhugashvili.

Hawsers are ropes for mooring.
The masses need radios so they won't be masses anymore.
There is a world inside the world.

The gut-shot man takes a long time dying.
There's never a dearth of reasons to shoot the President.
Stalin's name was Dzhugashvili.
There is a world inside the world.

2.
Does anybody here know the stupid truth?
I believe in everything.
Tomorrow, my brothers, the crippled child climbs the hill.

A word is also a picture of a word.
Thirty years with a fishbone in her throat.
Does anybody here know the stupid truth?

I'm sloven in my heart.
The best things shimmer with fear.
Tomorrow, my brothers, the crippled child climbs the hill.

He liked a woman with a freckled cleavage.
Saying the word "windage" to himself.
Does anybody here know the stupid truth?

Don't pee on my leg. I want the total truth.
Trotsky's name was Brownstein.
Tomorrow, my brothers, the crippled child climbs the hill.
I believe in the power of premonitions.
Men floating down in white silk.
Does anybody here know the stupid truth?
Tomorrow, my brothers, the crippled child climbs the hill.

3.
This was the true beginning.
I am all over the world.
But I am not consoled.

Mexico is a place where they understand.
The dead are in the room.
This was the true beginning.

Listen to me. I have a story to tell.
Someone was sitting inside his body.
But I am not consoled.

Who wants a President with a pigeon's heart?
We'll give everybody cancer.
This was the true beginning.

I am reciting a life and I need time.
I know what sickness looks like.
But I am not consoled.

A misty light around the President's head.
What is metal doing in his body?
This was the true beginning.
But I am not consoled.

DEBBI BRODY

Santa Fe Soul Cento

He lights two candles,
confuses a haunting and a blessing.
I mourn having passed so quickly,
grief a thread of blue tears,

poison pitted plums.
I couldn't find the glass case for my heart,
I pretend that what exists now is enough.

Widowed birds talk all morning,
with wings that of course represent time,
a million particles of particulate,
a field trip to the origins,
a vault or someone's dresser drawer.

Wrap a blessing around your curse,
it will travel further.
The queen will undrown herself,
become the hurricane.

Don't speak of things no one can believe in
on the corner of a heavy heart.
Spread wide, shaking the ground.
Make the Mardi Gras small enough
      so it fits under the table,
at rest where you began.
Resist drowning altogether,
light a candle.
Even your silence holds a sort of prayer.

We have been to many worlds,
helped God get his work done,
held our hands wide,
able to live in a world of beauty.

The bitter rosary has a beginning
        and an end,
a fringe of vulgar silence.
The sand makes music and yet
    my eyes don't hear,
my heart forms a new constellation.
I imagine I am a camera,
a moon that won't forgive.
We were burnt to a reusable equation,
want things so simple we have
        complicated everything.
Life is a truffle, banished to the kitchen,
replete with redheaded women,
whiplash of winter's tantrums,
the slow unrolling of another hot afternoon.

I ate a handful of the wet earth,
almost at the place where we began,
fresh clothes and fresh starts,
a sour prayer rocked endlessly on the
        naked promise of endangered time.

Dissolve into wisps of unlived out longing,
upside down ache, anchors of the useless.
The cauldron boils with fish beneath the ice,
a balm for left behind children
undone inside a pomegranate.

Contain yourself.
If you see a person in this tableau,
      let me know.
Don't go there,
meaning is air. Sit and wait
for the inside color of
the tree and the acorn.

Go backwards everyday,
put the ghost at ease,
delicate hummingbirds washed down
      with single malt.
The love of it has burgeoned beyond comprehension,
as unseen as an unpredictable future.

In death we are a scrim, a dark crane,
caricatures of God,
charcoal and wine,

God will move to the outside,
a prisoner studying Socrates,
another dawn orchestrating the East,
a big mess to clean up.

Your own stories circle back,
a certain measure of surrender.
All stories are swelling and we can't keep track
        of time
so I will make it up for you.

If you have a choice of two things and can't
        decide, take both.
Ground yourself in here, which is ragged and choking,
wake in the night at the least sound,
grow an extra hand to reach across,
fall to the moon, like honey to the big dipper,
unable to hold the moist thin syntax.
Don't be afraid of being in the middle,
promise to write about what is underneath.
Living is like being suspended in
        a sphere,
the entryway is not a meadow, but
a crusted nest outside the door.
The day flashes like a blade overhead,
grinding luscious words into blue cornmeal.

How many hours are falling out of time,
charged with a fruit from a different world,
a solar system riddled with fragrance,
broken ideas in a pile, stars that look like friends?

Iron is iron until it rusts,
not a trap, just a bit of giving way,

a line of dark coffee rum.
Cellos recognize the need to rust,
immune to the fading of memory.

Stories are the opposite of gravity.
Who will tell me anything as completely as you?
Your blood runs like a river, a short walk in the dark,

an inverse ripening of the soul.

BETH BROWNE

Junk Mail: A Found Poem

What a scraping paring affair
a carney rebellion
the barb snapping not starboard
but possibly in parabola starward

Since the room is dark
it can create only from memory.
Here is nature once more
overheard not schubert
an involvement arpeggio

And yet that mark
on the wall is not
a hole at all
a spate of words
self-preservation

KERRI BUCKLEY

There Was Only the Sound of the Sea

No two people have ever been so happy
Could we not have dined up here alone?
There was only the sound of the sea
It was very beautiful, very mysterious

Could we not have dined up here alone?
To the right and the left bushes of some sort
It was very beautiful, very mysterious
Heaven could never be sufficiently praised!

To the right and the left bushes of some sort
Mrs. Dalloway said she would buy the flowers
Heaven could never be sufficiently praised!
Never had any words been so vivid and so beautiful

Mrs. Dalloway said she would buy the flowers
It is strange how a scrap of poetry works in the mind
Never had any words been so vivid and so beautiful
June had drawn out every leaf on the tree

It is strange how a scrap of poetry works in the mind
On the further bank the willows wept
June had drawn out every leaf on the tree
But they beckoned: leaves were alive; trees were alive

On the further bank the willows wept
A thousand stars were flashing
But they beckoned: leaves were alive; trees were alive
To blaze among candelabras, glittering stars

A thousand stars were flashing
Are we going to the Lighthouse?
To blaze among candelabras, glittering stars
What does one mean by "the unity of the mind?"

Are we going to the Lighthouse?
No two people have ever been so happy
What does one mean by "the unity of the mind?"
There was only the sound of the sea

KERRI BUCKLEY

Sea and Sky

A far sea moves in my ear
surely the sky is not that color

Now the washed sheets fly in the sun
the pillow cases are sweetening

A far sea moves in my ear

Where once a day the light slowly widens and slowly
thins, the moon lays a hand on my forehead

Surely the sky is not that color

The comets have such a space to cross
These lamps, these planets falling like blessings, like flakes

A far sea moves in my ear

A disturbance in mirrors, the sea shattering its grey one
And now I foam to wheat, a glitter of seas

A far sea moves in my ear
Surely the sky is not that color

NAN BYRNE

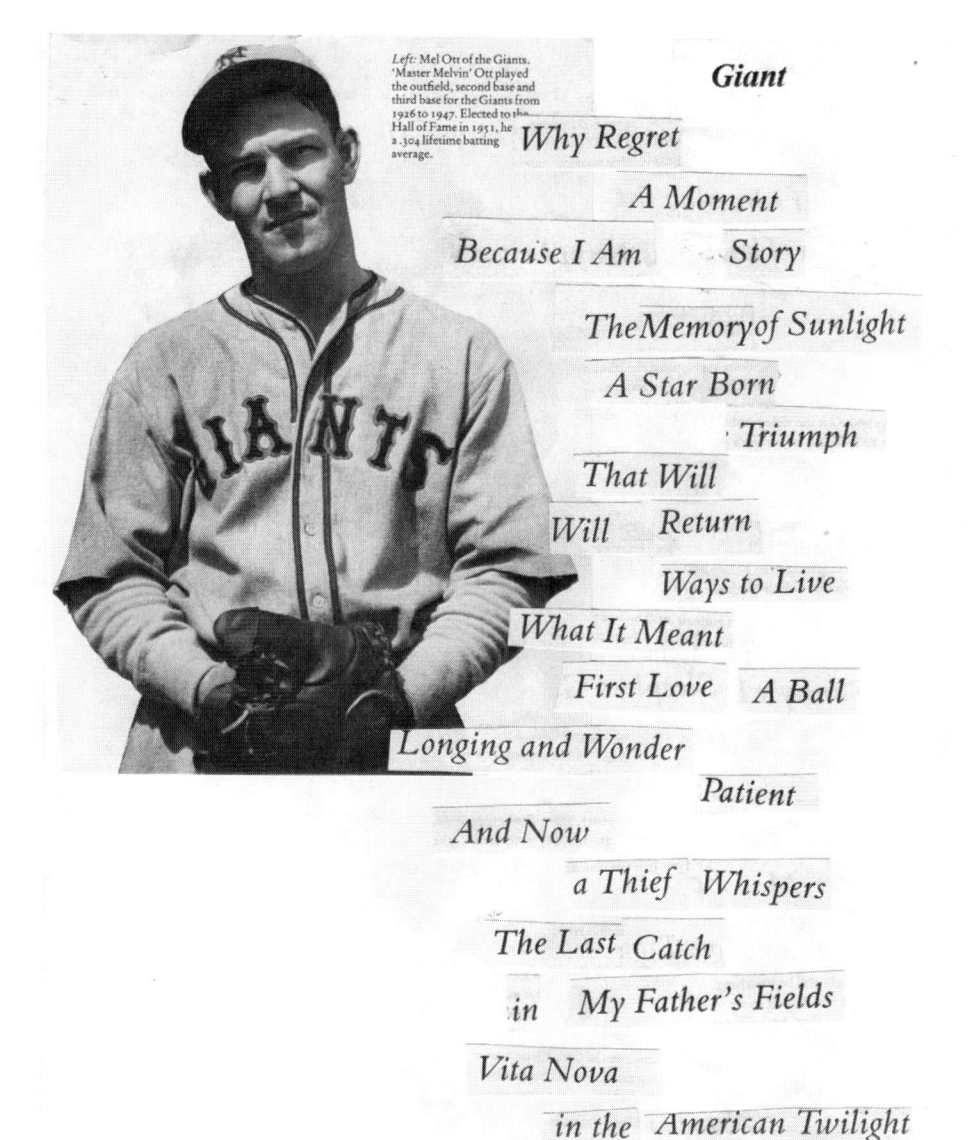

Left: Mel Ott of the Giants. 'Master Melvin' Ott played the outfield, second base and third base for the Giants from 1926 to 1947. Elected to the Hall of Fame in 1951, he a .304 lifetime batting average.

Giant

Why Regret

A Moment

Because I Am   Story

The Memory of Sunlight

A Star Born

Triumph

That Will

Will   Return

Ways to Live

What It Meant

First Love   A Ball

Longing and Wonder

Patient

And Now

a Thief   Whispers

The Last Catch

in   My Father's Fields

Vita Nova

in the American Twilight

Say You Love Me

CATHERINE CHANDLER-OLIVEIRA

I had some things

I had some things that I called mine—
I asked no other thing—
I lost a world the other day—
I years had been from home—

I thought that nature was enough—
I took one draught of life—
I watched the moon around the house—
I could not drink it, sweet—

I felt my life with both my hands—
I gave myself to him—
I could suffice for him, I knew—
I think I was enchanted—

I was a phoebe, nothing more—
I stepped from plank to plank—
I learned at least what home could be—
I am alive, I guess—

CATHERINE CHANDLER-OLIVEIRA

The Bard

Our hands are full of business: let's away,
and on our actions set the name of right;
with full bags of spices, a passport, too,
for we must measure twenty miles to-day
when day's oppression is not eased by night.
So come my soul to bliss, as I speak true.

If it appear not plain and prove untrue,
that so my sad decrees may fly away,
kill me to-morrow: let me live to-night!
Thou livest; report me and my cause aright.
Why didst thou promise such a beauteous day?
If thou say so, withdraw, and prove it, too.

Let me have audience for a word or two:
this above all: to thine ownself be true.
Yet I confess that often ere this day,
in cases of defence, 'tis best to weigh,
to look into the blots and stains of right,
in high-born words the worth of many a knight.

The mountain or the sea, the day or night—
one side will mock another; the other, too.
O, let me, true in love, but truly write
without all ornament, itself and true,
for fear their colours should be washed away,
as are those dulcet sounds in break of day.

The nightingale, if she should sing by day,
and she died singing it: that song to-night,
which by and by black night doth take away;
if she pertain to life, let her speak, too!
They would not take her life—is this not true?
O, blame me not, if I no more can write!

Never durst poet touch a pen to write:
we are but warriors for the working-day.
If what I now pronounce you have found true:
when the sun sets, who doth not look for night?
Please you, deliberate a day or two,
let thy fair wisdom, not thy passion sway.

There is no other way: do me this right—
and it must follow, as the night the day,
write till your ink be dry. O, 'tis too true.

ALEX CIGALE

How the Animals Came Into this World

When he comes, the moon
                asks him "Who are you?"
One answer passes
                muster: "I am you."
He who answers not
                becomes rain, falls down

and is born again
                as a worm or moth,
fish or bird, lion
                or a boar or snake,
or as a tiger,
                or as a person.

Men will not accept
                limit to their lives,
believe their pleasures
                should be limitless,
make their lives lethal
                grasping after wealth,

worry so about
               what they think they need
they never enjoy
               what they already have.
The real folly
               is their fear of death.

Men are asleep: when
               they die they awaken.
Keep these words, constant,
               foremost in your thoughts,
your hourly mantra:
               My health. It comes first.

TERESE COE

Clooth-na-Bare

Was it for this the wild geese spread,
And all that lamentation of the leaves?
Why, what could she have done, being what she is?
When all the wild summer was in her gaze.
And over the grave of Clooth-na-Bare,
The wind blows out of the gates of the day,
God stands winding His lonely horn,
And all that's beautiful drifts away:
A climbing moon upon an empty sky,
And Niamh calling Away, come away.

TERESE COE

Trifles

Come sing me a bawdy song, make me merry!
In nature there's no blemish but the mind,
Mad in pursuit and in possession so,
And therefore is winged Cupid painted blind.
From you I have been absent in the spring;
How like a winter hath my absence been.
What potions have I drunk of silent tears,
What freezings have I felt, what dark days seen!
Bid me discourse, I will enchant thine ear,
Gilding pale streams with heavenly alchemy.
Love is a spirit all compact of fire,
A snapper-up of unconsidered trifles,
Had, having, and in quest to have, extreme;
Before, a joy proposed, behind, a dream.

ALLAN DOUGLASS COLEMAN

Things to Remember about Shafting

I
What is a dynamo?
What is an eccentric?
How would you raise a shaft?
Why not more pressure?
Why is it lower?
Explain the cause of it.

II
How do you know when you have taken enough off?
Now what should be done?
Can you raise, lift, or suck hot water?
How is it done?
an you name the different pumps?

III
What is a cavity?
How does it act?
Why is it put there?
Why should it be so?

IV
How do you know when your pump is in good working order?
Why so?
What generally prevents a pump from working?

What are the different corrosions?
Of what use is a safety-valve?
How does it work?

V
What is a lubricator for?
How does it operate?
Would that not alter the length of the rod?
How much?
How would you do that?

VI
What would you do in case the eccentric slipped around on the shaft?
What is a cushion for?
Why does the adjustment make a difference?
How is it generally done?
Can the adjustment be made while running?
How should that be done?
By what name is the above known?

VII
What explosions are the worst?
What is meant by clearance?

PHILIP DACEY

Collage Sonnet: Thomas Eakins on Painting

Before you paint the sitter, paint the chair.
Get things as they are. Make a fat man fat.
Why should we copy Greeks? They copied nature.
The hand shaped right tells how to shape the foot.

Make it better or worse—never compromise.
Take an egg, or paper, and paint that shade of white.
Good pictures tell you what o'clock it is.
Remember, you're a portraitist of light.

An outline of a man is not a man.
Study math. Know bones. Don't paint when tired.
Devils sometimes live in colors. Facts *and*
vision. To paint the male or female nude,
first attempt a boat running with full sails.
Respectability in art appalls.

PHILIP DACEY

Patchwork Sonnet of Friends' Complimentary Closes

Riches, poverty, solitude, friendship.
Gold and potatoes. Visitations. Wings.
Peace, power, love, luck, cheers, and a safe trip.
May a thousand flowers bloom! All good things.
Salubrious catastrophes. Clarity.
Luego. Zdravo. Sayonara. Shalom.
Health, rage, and macadamia nuts. Let it be.
Yours till Reaganomics works. Hurry home.
Cherish folly. Seize that carp. Unscrew
the inscrutable. Hugs and slugs. Keep on. Adieu.
Hoka hey. Tra la. Adios. Hidee ho.
Mutter spiffy. Write. Tell me what you know.
Salt in your blood and wine in your glass. Ciao.
Take it easy but take it. Bye for now.

MARTHA DEED

Misunderestimated Will of Me in the Actual Unedited Words of George W. Bush: A Fabulous Year for Laura and Me (December 2001)

We need to counter the shockwave of the evildoer
We need to counter the shockwave of the evildoer
had we to do it all over again
had we to do it all over again
of the shockwave we had to do all over
we need the evildoer to counter it again

these hateful few who kill at the whim of a hat
these hateful few who kill at the whim of a hat
it's hard work
it's hard work
it's hard at the whim of work
these few who kill a hateful hat

We would look at the consequences of catastrophic success
We would look at the consequences of catastrophic success
All and all, it's been a fabulous year for Laura and me
All and all, it's been a fabulous year for Laura and me
fabulous success all me, and all we, and all would look at Laura
it's been in a year of consequences and for the catastrophic all

It's been a fabulous success for these consequences
all whim and shockwave in the year of Laura and me
we look at the need of all to work – the few who had it
we would kill a hateful evildoer over at the counter
it's all hard hat to do again
we all of catastrophic all

MARTHA DEED

River Road Cento: a Sevening

E-Z load Camel blow-out sale
fox hunts trail 5 days 'til Spring
no dumping fish on center lane

America's Choice by order of state fire marshal
complete from design to installation
a blessing on the man who puts his faith in God

16 signs of progress on River Road

SHARON DOLIN

Char'd Endings

Of ruined and transcendent lovers
There is no absence that cannot be replaced
In their carnivorous landscape
It's you my father who are changing
Leaning on your reflection in the window
Already the oil rises from the lead again
Beloved! Feel the dark planting waken
Woman breathes, Man stands upright
The earth loved us a little I remember
Like a horse aimless at his bitter plowing
Failure is of no moment, even if all is lost
Everything swoons into transiency
Keep us violent and friends to the bees on the horizon
Such is the heart
I hurt and am weightless

CAROL DORF

A Cento of Stolen Moments

The globe is pulverized by its reflections.
At any rate, this is easy to verify.
This fall you will taste carrots.
This hour is the way the trees are taken.

I looked at wheat and at river cities.
Luckily everything's changed now that I steal.
The patroller, disinterested, holds all the beans.
Here elsewhere; elsewhere, here: a glass block, a ball.

Here, where you left me alone,
Is where I first fell in love with unreality.
Separate the various parts of the condition,
Shifting from one foot to another.

With a decent happiness,
Only the ghost of Lady Day knows where.

CAROL DORF

You Had Meant to Catch It

So many guides who leave me in the lurch
They carelessly grow the fruit
bulging out of leaf mulch

How I longed to be the hero
compelled to sling paint by an empty space
that could not redeem him

What it threshed or cut, what it sewed
into the years of separation
scattered shoreline farms

A few coins, and a clock made of sand
All things grow rigid and bright,
we know we are provisional.

EDWARD DOUGHERTY

The Witness

In fear of death I sat up
clinging, sitting at least
was something alive: the dead
do not sit.
                They come to me
in the silence of the night.

                Want to see?
                      Reexamine all you have been told.
            Want to see?
                      Come forward and bear witness.

                        A witness struggles
                        not to flinch,
                        not to look away.

This requires effort
and love.

        Want to see?

There had been a pit there,
it was already filled in,
and blood . . .
like a geyser.

Beside me
there was a woman
with blue lips. She suddenly
came out of that trance
and whispered in my ear (everyone
spoke in whispers):
                Can you describe this?

Can you tell me why?

*How can they stand there
firing at children?*

                            Reexamine all you have been told.

                                    A witness struggles . . .

. . . effort and love . . .

Then:
to a big trench maybe a hundred
a hundred and eighty meters long,
and there was an enormous grating,
an iron grating.
There were corpses burning on it.

How is it possible?

     Come forward.

  Can you describe this?

The night was hot
and seemed hotter
because of the fires against the sky.

     Come forward.

I have realized
I have been victim
and executioner.

     Come forward.

Two young girls were badly burned
and had lost their families.
The younger one complained

she was cold. She began shivering
and again said it was cold.
She suddenly stopped
and was dead.

    What is it
that is missing
     in us?

>Come forward.

>>These are human beings.

>Come forward.

>>You share hunger and fear
>>like salt and blood.

>Come forward and bear witness.

>Can you describe this?
And I said *Yes, I can.*
And then
something like a smile
crossed what had been
her face.

Come forward:
a new courage:
I call it
rage.

LILA W. DUCKETT

A Villanella

The bolero, silk-tasseled, walks your dreams
All that black hair for the asking like oceans I have never seen
The fuschia scarf comes off

I would like to lose myself
Behind a curtain of dark breath
The fuschia scarf comes off
The bolero, silk-tasseled, walks your dreams

You are unbraiding small braids
Your face behind a curtain of dark breath
Your lids emerge
All that black hair for the asking like oceans I have never seen

It's time you learned something
Your breast, so tiny, wound
Now the couch is baring its red throat
The bolero, silk-tasseled, walks your dreams

There's no need to say anything
My heart is humming a tune
I haven't heard in years
All that black hair for the asking like oceans I have never seen

You must understand me
Your breasts echo all the breasts which cannot swell
Sadness is not enough
The bolero, silk-tasseled, walks your dreams
All that black hair for the asking like oceans I have never seen

ELLEN ELDER

My Mother's Ashes

I'd entombed her in my own breast.
Isn't it a terrible thing to die so young as that?
I went out barelegged at dusk and dug and dug and dug.
Because a woman's body
is a grave; it will accept anything.
And it asks nothing, a name tag, a few trinkets.
Idols and ambergris and rare inlays.
Since the dead do not like being alone.

The sound of water was in the room.
If it was only the outer voice of sky.
A woman drew her long black hair out tight.
She turned from me, as if death were catching.
Her blue garments unloose small bats and owls.
She was alone and still, gazing out to sea.
Why should I blame her that she filled my days with misery?

I had to forgive my own failure to perceive how things were:
The sea was not a mask. No more was she.
They carved her sweet hills out.
This time anorexia didn't deliver.
A beige, flat fish, around whom parasites, slices of lemon.
But how can hunger confer safety?
Hours, where something might have floated up.
Ashes to ashes. We all fall down.

Two girls in silk kimonos both
Beautiful, one a gazelle.
Shutting their mouths on it, like a Communion tablet.
(Have you ever put a butterfly in your mouth?)
It is hardly a feast.

Mother, I didn't forgive you.
It is my stomach that makes me suffer.
Whose language is hunger.
In the slow float of differing light and deep.
I have been flickering, off, on, off, on.
But I don't do it. I want to live.

Unreal forgiving. Show me your face in fury—
It would be hung in the attics . . . ; it would be destroyed.
Nobody watched me before, now I am watched.
And this was my worst guilt; you could not cure.
We live under the skin of language.

MARGARITA ENGLE

He Who Cannot Run Flies

Little white horse
take me away from here,
take me to the town
where I was born

At the gates of heaven
shoes are sold
for little angels
who are barefoot.

Peanuts,
the peanut man
is going away . . .

The cat has four feet
and can choose only one path.

Of musician, poet, and lunatic
we all have a little bit.

MARGARITA ENGLE

Fresh Produce Tabloid Headlines

Granny Smith dates wild rice.
Honey dressing rosemary.
Ginger sprouts baby basil.
Bitter mums cut daisy.
Jumbo nuts squash sweet potato eyes.
Virgin olive oils curry party favors.
Sherry capers in brine. Romaine heart halved.
Sage mangoes nuts, endive heads sliced.
Bunch of scallions snap beans.
Pink Lady apple for sale, mint.
Bamboo shoots sweet corn.
Oyster mushroom—pearl onion!

CARMINE ESPOSITO

In the Center of Furies

Singing out from their mothers toughness
Children set their clocks to listen at the tissue walls
While Detroit and Watts and San Francisco were burning
That promise had come again

But I who am bound by my mirror
I leave you guardian
Is not the most noteworthy star
Caught between history and obedience

Passing men in the street who are dead
And afraid
He toys with anger like a young cat
In a new place next to a river of blood

By the rising sea
Under a merciless white light
The night is full of messages
Like flowering mines

We are elementary forces colliding in free fall
Each one of us
Like the fabled memory of elephants
This land will not always be foreign

Beyond anger or failure
I speak without concern for the accusations

CARMINE ESPOSITO

Green Is the Night and Out of Madness Woven

I. A refrain from the end of the boulevards,
      Are sounds blown by a blower into shapes,
           A doctrine to this landscape. Yet, having just

Stripped one of all one's torments, concealed
      That such ferocities could tear
           The tongue, the fingers, and the nose

This arrival in the wild country of the soul,
      Smacks like fresh water in a can, like the sea
           The poison in the blood will have been purged,

The rusty, battered shapes
      Of the mind that forms itself
           Skims the real for its unreal

II. Without ideas in a land without ideas
      One would continue to contend with one's ideas.
           The sky is too blue, the earth too wide.

This great world, it divides itself in two,
      Too conscious of too many things at once,
           The law of chaos is the law of ideas

The whole of the wideness of night is for you,
      If the stars that move together as one, disband,
           Their brilliance through the lattices, crippled

This chaos will not be ended,
    It glares beneath the webs
        The blood-red redness of the sun,

III.   In the sum of the parts, there are only the parts.
        That elemental parent, the green night,
            Was less than moonlight. Nothing exists by itself.

    The deer and the dachshund are one.
        The hand between the candle and the wall
            And the river that batters its way over stones,

    What is it that my feeling seeks?
        The companion in nothingness
            Older than any man could be.

    The black wind of the sea
        The street lamps
            The world as word,

IV.   The moonlight crumbled to degenerate forms,
        Each drop a petty tri color. For this,
            The shadows lessen on the walls.

    And, like an insatiable actor, slowly and
        As if yesterday's people continued to watch
            We buried the fallen without jasmine crowns.

The mind is the great poem of winter, the man
        If, while he lives, he hears himself
                The actor that will at last declaim our end.

  The shadow of the pears
        No shadows of themselves.
                That's what misery is,

V.   Green is the night and out of madness woven,
        By a wind that seeks out shelter from snow. Thus
                It may be that the ignorant man, alone,

Held in his hand the suave egg-diamond
        One sparrow is worth a thousand gulls,
                And must be loved, as one loves that

On the ground, fixed fast in a profound defeat.
        At the neutral centre, the ominous element
                Became the form and the fragrance of things

The premiss from which all things were conclusions,
        After the final no there comes a yes
                In which we pronounce joy like a word of our own.

MARGARET FIELAND

Twelve Drummers Drumming: A Haiku Sequence

Twelve drummers drumming
When the snow was round about
Now the ground is white

Nine ladies dancing
Excavating for a mine
Dashing through the snow

Ten lords a-leaping
When the snow lay round about
Making spirits bright

Dashing through the snow
A partridge in a pear tree
Make the Yule-tide gay

If the Fates allow
When a poor man came in sight
Let your heart be light

And the store boss said
When a poor man came in sight
Jingle all the way!

ANNIE FINCH

Compassion for Scarpia

"Rain down, voluptuous stars!
Tosca is burning with love!"

(pulsing to stars as if she kept them shining

"God forgives me"

(pulsing with the hypocrisy of her faith)

(He stalks in and the music stops
to make room for the drums and horns
and for his wide-topped florid boots)

"He forgives me,
he sees that I'm weeping."

(singing to them as if she kept them shining
shining with the hypocrisy of her faith)

("I swore you'd be mine" strikes at the choir,
the fallen angel's bass so beautiful)

"You clung to your love,
agile as a leopard

clung as agile
as a leopard to your love
and in that moment

that moment I swore

you'd be
mine,

mine. Mine"

"Finally mine!"

(how will he bathe in compassion?)

"Finally mine!"

"That is Tosca's kiss!"

"Finally mine!"

(in compassion,
as in the waters of the pond?)

"That is Tosca's kiss!"

Trembled "tutta Roma"
(and all Rome trembled before him)

This is her passion: "Die!"

"Die! Look, it's me, Tosca!"

(how will she bathe in compassion?)

"Now in death I forgive him!"

(how will they bathe
in the waters of that pond?)

"Finally mine!"

"Now in death I forgive him!"

(green mist settles on the battlements,

on the thin harmonies of every flute)

"Mario, Mario: "Never have I loved life more"

"I'll close your eyes with a thousand kisses
soothe you with a thousand words of love"

When he is gone
the same footsteps come plodding through the shadows;

it is she at the edge of the dark and killing ritual.

SUSAN FIRER

Call Me Pier

I have just returned from a visit to my pier
For a long time I would go to pier early
So much depends upon a pier
This is an old pier
I celebrate my pier, and what I assume . . .
I had a pier
There is a certain slant of pier
On woman's first disobedience, and the pier
Christmas won't be Christmas without the pier
I wandered lonely as a pier
Pier was spiteful
This is just to say I have eaten the pier

RICHARD FLYNN

Men of Our Time

1.

Yesterday, I discovered my wife,
Tonight I cup your breasts,
Though she is only in the next room.
I love breasts, hard.
A frown gathers behind my wife's smile.
I have a delicious problem.

I waited eighteen years to become a man.
Dad told me to hold the knife,
Long before he thought of his own death.
I know many men who wouldn't.
Pollen from the goldenrod rises:
May there be an afterlife.

2.

My father entered the kingdom of roots,
A man clothed in memories.
He danced with tall grass,
He didn't like being caged up,
He cradled his head in those hands,
He wanted to need no one, not

My mother.
She gives a half-choked sob.
Mother I'm sure you remember
My first experience in a whorehouse—
I stayed out all night and was drunk;
Fifteen years later I still give thanks.

3.

I get these girly magazines in the mail, because
I have pried up, brushed off the self in me.
I walk into your house, a friend.
I stand before the window that opens.
August lightning opens the afternoon sky,
During "The Desires of Monique."

Ordinarily I call it "my cock," but
Complaint is often the result of an inefficient
Twitching in the cactus.
It nods
Into that pit
When I take off your red sweatpants.

JACK FOLEY

Valentine's Day Cento (Chaucer / Milton / Pope / Byron / Shelley / Baudelaire / Joyce): The Radio Changes Poet Channels

Endeth thanne love in wo? Ye, or men lieth!
Virtuous and vicious every man must be
A forster was he, soothly, as I gesse
When she hath lost it in hir wantownesse
She gives in large recruits of needful pride
I was to do my part from Heav'n assigned
Ask of the learned the way? The learned are blind
"I se," quod she, "the myghty god of Love"

When she hath lost it in hir wantownesse
What dire offence from amorous causes springs?
Satan from Hell scap't through the darksome Gulf
Prescribed her heights, and pruned her tender wing
Full swetely herde he confessioun
And plesaunt was his absolucioun

Her blood was not all Spanish, by the by
And the fair shape waned in the coming light!
Where wert thou, mighty Mother, when he lay
Like a pale flower by some sad maiden cherished—
When she hath lost it in hir wantownesse
O blake nyght, as folk in bokes rede,
That shapen art by God this world to hide

Tisn't only tonight you're anachronistic!
Grandfarthring nap and Messamisery and the knave of all knaves and the joker.
Heehaw!
She was just a young thin pale soft shy slim slip of a thing then, sauntering—

La Maladie et la Mort font des cendres de tout le feu—

Say, my heart's sister, wilt thou sail with me?
Bababadalgharaghtakamminarronnkonnronntonnerronntuonnthunntrovarrhounawnskawntoohoohoordenenthurnuk!

AUDREY FRIEDMAN

Cento (Mark Doty, *Atlantis*)

. . . and I can study all day in an element of color
a composition in twenty aspects of gray
nocturne in black and gold
sea lavender shivers
at the juncture of elements

a wide vocabulary of ornament
one vast conjugation of the verb to shine
cinnabar and verdegris
summer's deep watered greens
gleaming eggwhite

watered paint pours
is it a human soul the painter's poured
think abalone
the wildly rainbowed mirror of a soapbubble sphere
think sun on gasoline

turbulent stasis on a blue background
everything's yellow and blue—coastal colors
until they are refracted and reassembled
melting in—what would you call this color?
gorgeous disarray

hung on the edges of the page
like Chinese brushstrokes
it seems a field
of endless jade
the colors in old Woolworth's watercolor boxes

description is itself a type of travel
chartreuse fixed and fired here
in the cold, the world's glazes
pigment on unmarbled paper
frozen, galactic, held

KATE GALE

Did you ever dance with the devil in the pale moonlight?

The devil went down to Georgia looking for a soul to steal.
Lead us not into temptation but deliver us from evil.
Thine be the glory.

Underestimated from day one, you'd never think
I was the master of the universe, now would ya?
Satan came to him and said,
"If you are the Son of God, command these stones to become bread."

The rod of correction shall drive the foolishness out of a child.
The devil can cite Scriptures to his purpose.

I deal with temptation by yielding to it.
Ordinary morality is only for ordinary people.

DIANE GERSONI-EDELMAN

Cento: Falls the Shadow

If the day writhes, it is not with revelations.
Your doctrines blew like ashes from your bones
Sprawled in the bowels of the earth,
Preserved, obscene, to mock black flights of years.

Send out your signals, hoist
Your dark scribbled flags,
These tracings from a world that's dead,
So foul, the hovering buzzard sees it fair.

I play your furies back to me at night.
Across an autumn freezing everywhere,
Past fingered ridges and their shrivelling span,
The moonlight is laid like a drawn sword.

Perhaps the soul only puts out a hand.
Breath quickens, heart beats faster, till at last,
Echo of mine, I am amenable,
The mortal begging in the squandered sun.

DANA GIOIA

A Short History of Tobacco

Profitable, poisonous, and purely American—
it was Columbus who discovered it
on reaching China, noticing the leaves
on a canoe. He sent his men ashore
to find the Great Khan's palace. The returned
to tell of squatting natives who drank smoke.

Rolfe smuggled seeds to cold, bankrupt Virginia.
When he returned years later, all the streets
were planted with the crop, the marketplace
and churchyards overgrown. Grim ministers
preached harvest from the pulpit and stood out
among the fields at night to guard their tithes.

More valuable than silver, worth ten times
the price of peppercorn. In Africa
six rolls could buy a man. The ships would reach
Virginia stocked with slaves or English wives
while every year the farms moved farther west
abandoning their dry, exhausted fields.

Tenacious, fertile, rank as any weed,
Linnaeus counted forty thousand seeds
inside one pod. Miraculus, he wrote,
the cure for toothache, shingles, running sores
or pushed by bellows through a patient's lung,
the panacea of the alchemists.

Fragrant, prophylactic, and medicinal,
Pepys chewed it during the Great Plague.
It cost a fortune, but it saved his life.
Later he spent an afternoon to watch
a surgeon kill a cat with just one drop
of the quintessence of Virginia leaf.

. . . But when a bear was killed, tobacco smoke
was blown into his throat to soothe the spirit.
The elders smoked and chanted in a trance.
The Mayans blew the smoke to the four corners
of the world. It was a gift from God,
profitable, poisonous, and purely American.

DANA GIOIA

Elegy with Surrealist Proverbs as Refrain

"Poetry must lead somewhere," declared Breton.
He carried a rose inside his coat each day
to give a beautiful stranger—"Better to die of love
than love without regret." And those who loved him
soon learned regret. "The simplest surreal act
is running through the street with a revolver
firing at random." Old and famous, he seemed *démodé*.
There is always a skeleton on the buffet.

Wounded Apollinaire wore a small steel plate
inserted in his skull. "I so loved art," he smiled,
"I joined the artillery." His friends were asked to wait
while his widow laid a crucifix across his chest.
Picasso hated death. The funeral left him so distressed
he painted a self-portrait. "It's always other people,"
remarked Duchamp, "who do the dying."
I came. I sat down. I went away.

Dali dreamed of Hitler as a white-skinned girl –
impossibly pale, luminous and lifeless as the moon.
Wealthy Roussel taught his poodle to smoke a pipe.
"When I write, I am surrounded by radiance.
My glory is like a great bomb waiting to explode."
When his valet refused to slash his wrists,
the bankrupt writer took an overdose of pills.
There is always a skeleton on the buffet.

Breton considered suicide the truest art,
though life seemed hardly worth the trouble to discard.
The German colonels strolled the Île de la Cité—
some to the Louvre, some to the Place Pigalle.
"The loneliness of poets has been erased," cried Éluard,
in praise of Stalin. "Burn all the books," said dying Hugo Ball.
There is always a skeleton on the buffet.
I came. I sat down. I went away.

ANNE GORRICK

21st Century Girls: A Quarter-Cento

The world can't be a vampire forever,
the end will be hands, unbearably loud
of yellow boomvy as a D-cup
You streak, divine down Mulholland Drive—
moneyed enough
and it's difficult to make metaphor out of
the body's lower idle, the human purr
Sugah says, baby, come zip my dress
You have knife pleats in your skirt, a selfish
all pink like showing its tits
You're making noises like a husband
and he groped for her Volvo under the gauze
A boy is a girl with a strap-on
failings get rescripted as uncanny. her
who filled the trolly and washing machine, and wrote
and too wanton for ordinary chores.
Vastness writes into the space that was her
hem   simplify ardor and we
Metaphor makes thing equivalent
Like him I was getting paid to act like I believed
liquid without sun—at all, not on its rim.
I rhyme with the ground
Because she's in a body, it makes decisions.
Hope for the artist in America & etc
There is the sound of dust heard over the telephone

KATE GREENSTREET

eclipsed

ordinary sunlight

what heat
reveals

crash-prone
first bite
bright stuff

to acquire the sun

the crest
the ridge

a part of life called disappointment

look for the break
it's enough

glow brightly in a vacuum

I think we have that, don't you?
it's green

and
it's unpredictable

prominence

to explore the sun
just   sit   back

it's working
it's running

aroused a demand
raised fears
this trace
let's go

24 stop

KATE GREENSTREET

He learns he was given a secret name

He declines
He dreams
dying just a year

leaving his eye open

This politeness is
philosophy itself
It is especially not

a thin line

He writes his first
novel at age fifteen, about the theft
of a diary
He had a house on two floors

Saw their shadows
Literally
I saw their shadows

He doesn't care about life

He is looking for the other
life, all the time
Somebody come and whispered in his ears
Let me think

R. S. GWYNN

Approaching a Significant Birthday, He Peruses The Norton Anthology of Poetry

All human things are subject to decay.
Beauty is momentary in the mind.
The curfew tolls the knell of parting day.
If Winter comes, can Spring be far behind?

Forlorn! the very word is like a bell
And somewhat of a sad perplexity.
Here, take my picture, though I bid farewell,
In a dark time the eye begins to see

The woods decay, the woods decay and fall—
Bare ruined choirs where late the sweet birds sang.
What but design of darkness to appall?
An aged man is but a paltry thing.

If I should die, think only this of me:
Crass casualty obstructs the sun and rain
When I have fears that I may cease to be,
To cease upon the midnight with no pain

And hear the spectral singing of the moon
And strictly meditate the thankless muse.
The world is too much with us, late and soon.
It gathers to a greatness, like the ooze.

Do not go gentle into that good night.
Fame is no plant that grows on mortal soil.

Again he raised the jug up to the light:
Old age hath yet his honor and his toil.

Downward to darkness on extended wings,
Break, break, break, on thy cold gray stones, O sea,
And tell sad stories of the death of kings.
I do not think that they will sing to me.

KIMBERLY HAMILTON

Land of the Fairy Chimneys

Like the soft peaks of Italian meringue,
vast pinnacles of eroded volcanic ash
sculpted by wind and flood water
seem to defy gravity.

Treking the silk road and the spice road
to wander through the
rock formations and Byzantine churches,
gypsy people follow the path of their ancestors.

Almond trees dressed in autumn colors,
houses and dovecotes carved into stones,
monasteries, churches and underground cities—
a whole city of dwellings carved.

MARYANNE HANNAN

An American Cento

With Malice toward None, Charity for All
Remember the Alamo
All Men Are Created Equal
A Full Dinner Pail
E Pluribus Unum
The War to End War
We Have Just Begun to Fight
 From Sea to Shining Sea
Happy Days Are Here Again
Fourscore and Seven Years Ago
Mine Eyes Have Seen the Glory
We Hold These Truths to Be Self-evident
I'm a Yankee Doodle Dandy
Give Me Liberty or Give Me Death
A Chicken in Every Pot
Tippecanoe and Tyler Too
United We Stand; Divided We Fall
New Deal
This Land Is Your Land

Ask Not What Your Country Can Do for You
Live Free or Die
A Public Office Is a Public Trust
Government of the People, by the People, for the People
Excelsior
I Have a Dream
Pike's Peak or Bust
Leave No Child Behind
We Want Wilkie
He Serves His Party Best Who Serves His Country Best
Speak Softly and Carry a Big Stick
Manifest Destiny
No Taxation Without Representation
Life, Liberty and the Pursuit of Happiness
Don't Fire Till You See the Whites of Their Eyes
A Thousand Points of Light
Oh, Say, Can You See
When Johnny Comes Marching Home Again

MICHAEL HANNER

On Finding a Book of Poems

At first it was going to be a book of poems
lighter than the shimmering popular leaves.
Today I stop myself;
my earliest memory is of standing alone.

Poetry is religion happening somewhere
on this early summer night.
If I were to write about you,
would flesh re-attach to bone?

If I were free to write this poem
exactly as I chose,
when I awake in the morning I am seven,
in my mother's complete holding.

Along the margins of invincible day: recognition.
My mother was in the moon tonight.
I feel her skull
and the shape of her face beneath the skin.

Hours inland she sits at her kitchen table
dreaming an ocean of storms.
Now and then I break
as if my heart knew something terrible.

I found the rings in a box.
I find teeth at the bottom of the garden.
I've been up a long time.
There are times when my skin darkens.

See the smoke in this photograph?
Ghostly shapes hover in the air.
Our tribe may be down to two
 so we sit here, holding hands.

The Monarchs have returned.
The heat has broken.
The prairie is a window open;
far away a woman dances.

BARBARA HANTMAN

Burns Festschrift

Amang the brachens, on the brae,
      Between her an' the moon,
O my Luve's like a red, red rose,
   That's newly sprung in June.

To adore thee is my duty,
      Goddess o' this soul o' mine!
Thy crystal stream, Afton, how lovely it glides.

There's wild-woods grow, and rivers row,
What signifies the life o' man,
     An' 'twere na for the lasses, O.

Naething could resist my Nancy:
I kiss'd her owre and owre again,
     Amang the rigs o' barley.

The best-laid schemes o' Mice an' Men
    Gang aft a-gley,
And we'll tak a cup o' kindness yet,
    For auld lang syne.

BARBARA HANTMAN

Gwendolyn Brooks: Medley of Wisdom

The boiling of an egg is heavy art.
You come upon it as an artist should,
With rich-eyed passion, and with straining heart:
Two who are Mostly Good,
Remembering, with twinklings and twinges,
Guards upon the heart to halt love
That runs without crookedness.

She was interested in a brooch and pink powder and a curl—
Therefore she terminated her mourning,
Made for her mouth a sad sweet smile.

Does he hunch up, as I do,
Against the dark of night?
Cutting across the hot grit of the day,
Warning that we are each other's harvest,
We are each other's magnitude and bond.

They took my lover's tallness off to war,
To court coquettish death, whose impudent and strange
Possessive arms and beauty (of a sort)
Live not for battles won,
Live not for the-end-of-the-song—
Live in the along.

Everybody here is infirm.
Oh. Mend me. Mend me. Lord.
Look! I am beautiful, beautiful with
My wing that is wounded:
The sun slappers,
The self-soilers,
The harmony-hushers—
What a pity what a pity. No love
For one so loving.

If Thou be more than hate or atmosphere
Step forth in splendor—
Mortify our wolves!

H. L. HIX

Letter to Dana Gioia

—Upon the publication of Disappearing Ink

Poets have a weakness for refrains,
the magnificently private language
of a poem balanced between two lives,
two sides of an enduring dialectic.

Poetry is a vast and flexible art,
no single intelligence or program
but a pervasive, permanent desire
to reinvent each manner from within.

Poets have a weakness for refrains,
corrections, deletions, fragments, dead ends,
pieces of Venetian stage machinery
isolated from literary life.

The hand of the poet reaches out
to join the incalculable holdings,
nourishing but unconventional
imaginative possibilities.

Poets have a weakness for refrains,
compressed, cranky, and cryptic letters from
deep-rooted, primitive human desire,
the irresistible force of poetry.

Who would not wish the poet a better fate?
Fear, guilt, and suffering cast their shadows,
a vast unarticulated landscape
of so many differing persuasions.

Poets have a weakness for refrains,
brief and mildly obscene obiter dicta,
clichés, proper nouns, foreign words, brand names
in the author's small meticulous hand.

I offer this welter of anecdote
brokered, built, and administered elsewhere:
cloaks, missals, rosaries, belts, and shoe leather,
as much as possible of what happened.

Poets have a weakness for refrains,
compressed, lyrical, and imagistic
assertions of personal preference
suffused with a sense of the sacred.

You'll have to address what's happening.
It is time to ask different questions,
clear expression and careful observation
transforming the factional politics.

Poetry is a vast and flexible art,
the harsher side of reality,
a comprehensively annotated,
abiding, unreasonable obsession.

Poets have a weakness for refrains,
a shared sympathy or mutual sense,
mostly syntactical, not logical,
of how we can win against the poem.

The language is still luminously clear
emotional sense of this alien place.
A word is the sum of its history,
objectified and indeterminate.

The years of silence and isolation:
who would not wish the poet a better fate?
Passion overcomes its possessor.
Poetry is a vast and flexible art.

H. L. HIX

Letter to Philip Brady

—Upon the publication of To Prove My Blood

Clanking through plaster labyrinths, shouldering fire,
    the body fades, not into love.
No, working here, no murmurs beyond ambition,
    I do not want to drown or burn.
Resurrection could redeem perfect forgetting.
    How, I don't know—more proof of guilt.
Walking mute and outlawed, dizzied in the whirlwind,
    the body fades, not into love.
It receded from the infinite, a small flame
    I have inherited, two ghosts
clanking through plaster labyrinths, shouldering fire.
    What's flesh anyway, without her?
Flailing in midlife, poised to dissolve, smothered now,
    I do not want to drown or burn.
Left to unspool, even brooding spirits breathe bones,
    and view from a great height the world,

ourselves becoming more visible day by day,
        light-headed for an afternoon
released into emergency when all are dead.
        I have inherited two ghosts,
shadowing behind them the untrustworthy air,
        dead people's mail, tree, explosion,
ocean, a little trouble, this watery tongue,
        a goddess to tell this story,
clanking through plaster labyrinths, shouldering fire.
        I do not want to drown or burn
this dwindling legacy, alleys and spires and birds,
        stars and pythons, my link to myth.
I must tell myself dust clouds, the shirr of that touch,
        and view from a great height the world.

JANIS BUTLER HOLM

A Magazine of Bare, Naked Ladies

Look on this wonder! / The sprawl and fullness of babes, the bosoms / the bending forward / and backward / the / perfect, varied attitudes /

You linger to see / love-flesh / lost in the cleave of / in the heave of / immeasurable / massive / naked / bosoms

There swells / softly / the naked meat of the body / there all / desires, reachings / the glory and sweet of / wildest largest passions /

O / to be with / to be surrounded by beautiful, curious, breathing / flesh / all the belongings of / a woman /

O / to be / whispering / reclining, embracing / teeming / shouting aloud /

O / deliciously aching / exquisite senses /

O / love!

JANIS BUTLER HOLM

Exercises in Subordination

1. A favorite diversion was hunting. A favorite diversion was hawking. These were diversions of the Middle Ages. They occurred at intervals. They occurred during the intervals of war.

2. We should suit our behavior to men. We should suit it to the several degrees of men. Of these degrees, there are three. We should suit our behavior to our superiors. We should suit it to our equals. We should suit it to those below us. This is the principal point of good breeding.

3. The Indian wife sailed with her husband for England. She sailed in 1616. She had been instructed in the English language. She bore an English name. She was "the first Christian of her nation."

4. Edward Plantagenet was the eldest son of King Edward III. He was born at Woodstock, in 1330. He was commonly called the Black Prince. He was called the Black Prince from the color of his armor. The color of the armor was specially chosen. It set off the fairness of his skin and hair.

5. The battle of Bunker Hill was fought on the 17th of June. It was fought in the year 1775. It proved the bravery of the Americans. It was followed by great moral results.

6. The natives of Virginia seized on a quantity of gunpowder. It was their first seizure of gunpowder. They sowed it for grain. They expected to reap a plentiful crop of combustion. They expected to reap this by the next harvest. They expected a crop so plentiful as to blow away the whole colony. The gunpowder seized by the natives belonged to the English colony.

7. To behold the peasantry is a pleasing sight. To behold them in their best finery is a pleasing sight. Their ruddy faces are pleasing. Their modest cheerfulness is delightful. To see them on a Sunday morning is a pleasing sight. To see them thronging tranquilly along the green lanes to church is most pleasant. At the time of their going the bell is sending its sober melody across the quiet fields.

8. The fowls of the earth furnish sustenance to man, and the beasts of the field furnish sustenance to man, and the dwellers of the deep furnace furnish sustenance to man.

9. It is a sad thing to be born a sneaking fellow. It is much worse than to inherit a hump-back. It is worse than to inherit a couple of club-feet. Looking upon such a fellow causes me sometimes a peculiar feeling. The feeling tells of the necessity of our loving the crippled souls. May I be allowed to use the expression "crippled souls"? We should love them with a certain tenderness. This tenderness we need not waste on noble natures.

MIKHAIL HOROWITZ

The Second Coming of the New Colossus

Turning and turning in the widening gyre
The falcon cannot hear the falconer;
Things fall apart; the centre cannot hold;
Mere anarchy is loosed upon

> *A mighty woman, with a torch whose flame*
> *Is the imprisoned lightning, and her name,*
> *Mother of Exiles. From her beacon-hand*

The blood-dimmed tide is loosed, and everywhere
The ceremony of innocence is drowned;
The best lack all conviction, while the worst

> command
> The air-bridged harbor that twin cities frame.
> Keep, ancient lands, your storied pomp! cries she
> With

A gaze blank and pitiless as the sun,

> Send me your tired, your poor,
> Your huddled masses

vexed to nightmare by a rocking cradle,
And what rough beast, its hour come round at last,
Slouches toward Bethlehem to

> lift my lamp beside the golden door.

MIKHAIL HOROWITZ

Twenty Couplets

1

Ha! Whare ye gaun, ye crowlin ferlie?
Half a league, half a league, half a league onward

2

Out of the cradle endlessly rocking,
From my mother's sleep I fell into the State

3

How many dawns, chill from his rippling rest
Could frame thy fearful symmetry?

4

I placed a jar in Tennessee,
Will you marry it, marry it, marry it.

5

Hog Butcher for the world,
Beside the rivering waters of, hitherandthithering waters of,
      Night!

6

A thing of beauty is a joy forever:
America I've given you all and now I'm nothing.

7

If "compression is the first grace of style,"
Better to reign in Hell than serve in Heaven.

8

I measure every grief I meet
My little horse must think it queer

9

Life, like a dome of many-colored glass,
—dipping into Death like a soup.

10

She walks in beauty, like the night
Scuttling across the floors of silent seas.

11

Oh, to be in England
                                      As far as Cho-fu-sa.

12

The ploughman homeward plods his weary way
In human gore imbued.

13

My father moved through dooms of love
When the plunging hoofs were gone.

14

In Xanadu did Kubla Khan
Rage, rage, against the dying of the light.

15

I wander'd lonely as a cloud
And made the kites to whet their beaks clack clack.

16

How do I love thee? Let me count the ways.
Tick, tick, tick, what little iambics

17

The punk I skorne and the cut purse sworn
BUT MY BONES ARE FUSCHIAS

18

What lips my lips have kissed, and where, and why,
Fall, gall themselves, and gash gold-vermilion.

19

A Book of Verses underneath the bough,
After hangin' Danny Deever in the mornin'.

20

Lulla, lulla, lullaby, lulla, lulla, lullabye
Boomlay, boomlay, boomlay, boom!

DARREN JACKSON

At the Hour of Love and Blue Eye Lids

I

It was a lavender blouse
Hiding nothing in the deep blue
Betwixt damnation and impassioned clay.

All look and likeness caught from earth
Only because behind it the sky is a doubtful, a doubting
In its own cloudless, starless lake of blue.

(We are as clouds that veil the midnight moon.)

When the mind's wings o'erspread
That pale, serrated indigo on the sea line,
Your white face turned away;

I weep; and walk endless ways of thought
Through the narrow doorway into the sunlight
Dwindled into a ghost not fit to cope.

The last memory I have,
Of aught on that illumined face,
Is sicklied o'er with the pale cast of thought.

But the south wind blows the sky clear at times
And, oiled and scented, urges you on
To feel in sad amazement then
The fool's gold of the sun.

II

Our face like a crumpled sheet
Then the space where the face has gone and the gaze remains
Where nothing can erase it,
The screaming face it was before it cracked,

Poised, unanswerable. If it is without
Measuring the full cadence of bare
Cobble of milky way
That leaves bright flesh like sand and turns it chill,

Then would I bear it, clench myself, and die.
And open to the bright and liquid sky,
Moon of a hundred equal faces
Where the ordinary hornets in a human's heart

Reveal the crimson flower flash
Tumbling like a waterfall of China silk,
Autumn and silk and nothingness. . .
Give me a thousand kisses. Then a hundred. . .

But I know better. When desolation comes,
Clouds take any shape they fancy.
But whose is this vapid face
Where the illusion of hope means skin torn from boxes?

III

It was not dark at first, that opening onto the red sea humming
The white ink of clouds,
Each with the scalped face of the other,
The white cobwebs and the dust on the eyelashes.

Above the end of the sky of my dreams
The light moves slowly past morning to afternoon
While even the wish to be
Melting snow, forest, rushes, river and boats
Returns, on unshod pale and coughing horses, descending the ladder of

Red birds new grass a yellow chair—
Heart of the ice-light emptiness, live, intense—
The poem of the mind in the act of finding
A clear curve of stone, mottled by stars
Swathed in exotic finery, in loose silks.

And when darkness folds this day
Empty, so that, before the other Empty, a
Ringing like the voices of birds, in very grave distress,

All the resources the tongue braids
Are unclenched. It is night. Songs have blossomed
With a thread of moonlight.

IV

For poetry makes nothing happen: it survives
Like the bird bones on the beach
The salt of the bay had worked on for a season.
Empty perfection, as I take you in
Under the incalculable sky, listless, diseased with stars
(and the wind whipped my throat),

Something startles me where I thought I was safest:
Perhaps half out of some speechless hope,
He battles heart and arm, his own blue sky
Of my skull shell of sky and earth
Already half a spirit, mumbling and muttering sadly
From the tangled web of thought and sinew.
In my heart, a scatter like milkweed.
Later thousands of dreams
Loosen the cord of years:
Long live the weeds that overwhelm
The green sky from which rain was falling;
And beyond it the deep blue air, that shows,

Through deserts of erotic flowers,
The carmine printed mouth.

V

Nothing has remained for me except language:
The fire red forehead—unconsumed by
The lips of those whose lips
Broke into a cataract
Then faded, and to follow them I burn'd
An urnful of ashes. Divine Poet! Did the pyre's flames
Quiet the barking distances?

Now that the moon, who remembers and only cares
That we arrive here improvised,
Is almost down, an answering gold
That leaped through the dark,
Observe the swelling turf, and say:
*You could lose your heart
In the dark blue kiss,*

*And the turning disk preserves, longer even,
The trace of a bird in snow* (as always
Knowing in you, that we do not exist)—
Enough! Enough! It is enough for me,
The frail duration of a flower:
Come hither in your shining purple gown.

TROY JOLLIMORE

Rosencrantz and Guildenstern Are Dead, Ruined by Reading the *Cantos* of Ezra Pound

—Or, Song of My Shelf

1

Under the volcano
in the garden of the North American martyrs
two serious ladies
left out in the rain
repair
the crooked timber of humanity.

2

God knows
love is the crooked thing.
God knows
the heart never fits its wanting.
God knows
the information:
all things, all at once.
God knows
the untouchable
dreams of distant lives.

3

When one has lived a long time alone
on the great Atlantic rainway,
and the stars were shining,
the importance of what we care about
lies
with ignorance,
divine comedies,
difficult loves.

4

Why, Brownlee left
The Book of Laughter and Forgetting
at Swim-two-birds.
Ulysses annotated
The Annotated Lolita
at weddings and wakes.
Praise
the cunning man,
the engineer of human souls.
Praise
the dispossessed,
the man who mistook his wife for a hat.

5

While England sleeps,
Kant and the platypus
kiss in the Hotel Joseph Conrad.
The boy on the step
second guesses
the fortunate traveller.
After Ovid,
who will run the frog hospital?

6

The world as I found it—
the world at large—
points, in time,
to the wedding:
a vision
of love and shadows,
first love and other sorrows.

7

What is justice?
A guide for the perplexed.
A thought in three parts.

A dream of mind.
The heart is a lonely hunter
on a cold road:
blizzard of one.
Must we mean what we say?
The horse's mouth
lies.
Consider the oyster.

8

If on a winter's night a traveler,
coming into the country
on a pale horse,
opening the hand
the rest of the way
for the union dead,
travels
with ignorance
of love and other demons,
love and its place in nature,
seeing things—
home truths,
signals of distress—
as if
the half-life of happiness
is 5,

as if
the world is the home of love and death—
if on a winter's night a traveler
travels,
can you stand to be blessed?
Can you hear, bird,
what we owe to each other?

9

Little friend, little friend,
fall on your knees.
Let it come down.
Call it sleep.

GENEVIEVE KAPLAN

133

wave him goodbye,
wanting a woman not wanting a woman,
    with a man
        a little sick with herself drying up and sitting

      the girl must run faster, look
      a girl can listen with her mouth

GENEVIEVE KAPLAN

166

Good the night came now;
seeing the bare branches they cried and laughed;
     I am not a child
    The day came wide
        good the first snow,
          She closed her mouth
            like the clock
      and the next day Fall

JEN KARETNICK

Centoum for Gin and Pilgrims

Welcome to Plymouth, twinned with tonic,
land of soap and glory.
Shake the bottle, wake the taste.
Embarkation and disembarkation only.

Land of soap and glory.
As one small candle may light a thousand,
embarkation and disembarkation only—
no permanent mooring.

As one small candle may light a thousand,
so the light kindled here has shone to many
no permanent mooring.
Smoking forbidden after this point.

So the light kindled here has shone to many:
Shake the bottle, wake the taste;
smoking forbidden after this point.
Welcome to Plymouth, twinned with tonic.

DIANE KENDIG

On Frida Kahlo's *Diego on My Mind*

The window square whitens and swallows its dark stars,
the weeping woman goes weeping along the river banks
Shall she not find comfort in the sun?
At night, she holds his pillow to her ribs and rubs.
(Memory, that preposterous and unreliable refuge
of things once loved and taken for granted.)
But how to speak to a man who does not see you,
who sees ogres, satyrs, perhaps the depth of hell itself?
He does not look up into the ever-changing expanse of morning.
Your health is bound to be affected if, day after day,
you say the opposite of what you mean.
Love, chimed the saints and angels.
Hate, shrieked the gun-metal princess.
Marriage could be the caption.
What is there to know?
Some shape of beauty moves away the pall.

TRACEY KNAPP

Blonde

lipstick on the cucumbers   she couldn't keep her calves together

male gets delivered to the right box   she wasn't used to being in the front seat

bite marks on the steering wheel   why was she upset

when her tampon is behind her ear   she can't find her pencil   fired from her job

why did the blonde fail   call the welfare office   jump off a bridge

drive into the ditch   why did she scale the chain-link fence   break her leg

marks on her back   how did the blonde explain   have another beer

other guys waiting their turn   the more you bang it

how many does it take to screw   a blonde at a flashing red light

crawling across the street   when is it legal to shoot a blonde in the head

couldn't dial 911   when she wakes up on the floor

she gets dressed and goes home

PHYLLIS KOESTENBAUM

What Would I Do Without This World Faceless Incurious: A Cento

When Abraham Lincoln was shoveled into the tombs:
After such knowledge, what forgiveness.
Because language dreams in metaphors,
Like a thirst for salt, for my childhood river, I arise,
I face the sunrise, never to kill myself.
I hate them, as I hate sex—
But I was going to say when Truth broke in
Mine was the weight
Of every brooded wrong, the hate—
I must be mad, or very tired; the dead heat rises for weeks.
O wind, rend open the heat,
Cut apart the heat . . .
Galileo, how are you?
You are the underside, thinking
Them persons was delighted.
Others will see the islands large and small.
Cold, uncertain of all.
You're on top. You call the shots.
There is no shape more terrible than this—
What is there to know?
A rat crept softly through the vegetation
Like ancient wallpaper.
Life, friends, is boring,
Dour and dark against the blinding snowdrifts.
Still I'm alive on the Abraham Lincoln swing.
I have mystical visions and cosmic vibrations.
It is 1959 and I go get a shoeshine—

Now you are laughing.
O sweet spontaneous!
I am black and I have seen black hands, millions and millions of them.
I think I may well be a Jew:
Men kill for this, or for as much.
Even then I have nothing against life; I came to explore the wreck.
Have you thought O dreamer it may be all maya, illusion?
Walking naked, this is not vanity.
"Love, O Careless Love."
I weep like a child for the past.

YALA KORWIN

Let the Snake Wait

Let the snake wait under
his weed
he has nothing else to do,
and the writing
can wait too.
Unless it prefers
to strike
like a snake
sleepless
like me.

The writing needs
through metaphor to reconcile
us—you and me.
Saxifrage is my flower that splits
the rocks.
You prefer lily's purity, so let it be.

JANE K. KRETSCHMANN

Volatile Territories

I am obliged to confess
that my sister Fanny,
with the express authority
of the caliph, has been abducted
for speaking out for women's
suffrage and against the slaughtering
of animals. The objective
of the abduction clothes its form
in a furious and satanic invective
against her selective solitude.
It is now that legend and history
become inextricably mixed.
Clearly the conquest of my sister
was a complicated sequence
of events. The report of her abduction
encountered public apathy,
but the legislature moved to
enlarge the insane asylum.

DAVID LEHMAN

December 14

This bed thy center is, these walls, thy sphere,
The tarnished, gaudy, wonderful old work
Of hand, of foot, of lip, of eye, of brow,
That never touch with inarticulate pang
Those dying generations—at their song.
The One remains, the many change and pass
The expiring swan, and as he sings he dies.
The earth, the stars, the light, the day, the skies,
A white-haired shadow roaming like a dream
Limitless out of the dusk, out of the cedars and pines,
Think not of them, thou hast thy music too—
Sin and her shadow Death, and Misery,
If but some vengeful god would call to me,
Because I could not stop for Death,
Not to return. Earth's the right place for love.
My playmate, when we both were clothed alike,
Should I, after tea and cakes and ices,
Suffer my genial spirits to decay
Upon the bridal day, which is not long?
I thought that love would last forever; I was wrong.

DAVID LEHMAN

Touchstones

That, in Aleppo once, where
With nectar pure his oozy locks he laves,
Bloom, O ye amaranths! Bloom for whom ye may,
Till elevators drop us from our day . . .

And would it have been worth it, after all,
To let the warm love in
Or stain her honor or her new brocade
To a green thought in a green shade?

As though to protect what it advertises,
Surely some revelation is at hand;
My music shows ye have your closes,
And to die is different from what anyone supposed, and luckier.

Blind mouths! as from an unextinguished hearth,
Me only cruel immortality
Consumes: whatever dies was not mixed equally
But does a human form display

Alone and palely loitering, like a rose rabbi.
O could I lose all father now! for why
I wretch lay wrestling with (my God!) My God,
Honey of generation had betrayed.

These modifications of matter into innocent athletes
Whose action is no stronger than a flower
Through Eden took their solitary way.
I, too, dislike it. With rue my heart is laden.

If you are coming down through the narrows of the River Kiang,
Where knock is open wide,
Fear death by water. To begin the morning right,
The small rain down can rain

Where ignorant armies clash by night
Though I sang in my chains like the sea.
Nor law, nor duty bade me fight,
Nor, in thy marble vault, shall sound

Joy's grape, with how sad steps, O Moon,
With naked foot stalking in my chamber.
The dark italics it could not propound,
And so—for God's sake—hock and soda-water!

KAREN LEWIS

Caught by the Light: A Cento

Hello, hello.

One woman leads to another,
the chandeliers aren't talking.

Who sends us these messages,
oblique and muffled,
for those who listen with their eyes,
tell me what it is for?

Confess: it's my profession.

The words I clench—
words fertilize each other,
language of the roots of rushes tangled,
mouth full of juicy adjectives.

I am amazed.
I am snow and
space, pathways.

We follow you
scattering floral tributes,
we are learning to make fire
(tanuluk tuzet rakni),
magic.

There is not much
time and time is not
fast enough for us any more,
traffic shifts back.
If we make stories for each other,
you make them new each time,
you trying to think of something
you haven't said,
making use of what
there is.

We need each others'
breathing, warmth, surviving,
is the only war
we can afford.

Call it Please. Call it Mercy,
of ink, twisting out into the clearness.
The steel question—
mark turns and opens,
where do the words go?
What can I give her?

Years ago you were caught by the light,
cut out of magazines
in another land.

It would be so good if you'd
believe,

the publicity.
The relationship is symbiotic,
indispensable.

At the last
judgment we will all be trees.

MARY LYON

That Would Be All of It

The cause was heart failure,
underneath, a feeling of bewilderment.
Married twice, once to a man named Bacchus,
Mrs. Ryan liked to sew dolls and soft toys.
She sought enduring love a little ambivalently.
I had to exist apart from them.
The trick is not to get frightened.
When you're dancing, don't look down at your feet.

Life unfolded as a kind of scroll.
His book was not as realistic as mine.
This was just a story to him.
He had been unable to hunt down only one flower he sought.
More than once he had to be talked down from a bridge,
sending out what he called a briefer signal.
The odds of survival can be almost insurmountable.

I thought the whole point was that we wouldn't feel stranded.
In my innocence I wanted to know everything,
have the courage to travel to those dimly lit spaces,
the idea of creating a new shadow on earth.
It started as a lark but ended as an ostrich.
I got tired of passing the houses of my dead friends.
They did not always wind up where they intended.

MIKE MAGGIO

A Muscle Disease, a Stream of Clear, Pure Water All Dried Up

one day
he combed the streets:
the prison plantation
reformed by incarceration

cubist waifs
haunting the pages
armed men
who chased and beat them
mankind's new design

tormented by extreme hunger and thirst
my first instinct was to jump out of bed
the huge trees all dried up and withered

we were born in this land
twelve years ago
a source of superprofits
obsessed with food and drink

now
the water has all dried up
the last human beings
tempering their strings
with all sorts of objects:
nails screws rubber bands
paper clips clothespins

once
the slaves were all happy
the daily bang-bang
the half-destroyed apartment buildings
purged of all life

then
a greenhouse worker in germany
issued risky bonds

everyone is now beautiful
pray all night without falling asleep
but there are no guarantees

there I sat on the toilet
a ghost harpsichord
a prime site for cultural fantasy
a junk bond
gut-wrenching, powerful and undeniable
we were born in this land:
center of immorality and vice
it's no news
flesh goes off   flesh goes on
overt torture is the norm
industrial slavery conducted under the whip
to keep the public out
the world of darkness

the before-death experience
an even more appalling
river of prison

if you want it now   you can get it.
the epoch of spontaneous mutation
damage to the nervous system
it does not always yield a reasonable answer

because almost every
america has become
a harbinger of sorts
the uncontested world leader
surrounding mecca and madina
persia, egypt, turkey and north africa

and so
the final meaning of music may now be suggested:
value per share = $D(K - g)$
$\qquad\qquad$ = a stream of clear, pure water
$\qquad\qquad$ = this morsel of gossip
wrought by human hands

MARTIN McGOWAN

Poetics

Terence, this is stupid stuff—
Excite the membrane, when the sense has cooled
To consecrate the flicker, not the flame.

The Moving Finger writes, and, having writ,
A gang of labourers on the piled wet timber
Babble, babble; our old England may go down in babble at last.

Do you remember Mr. Goodbeare, the carpenter,
Bent on writing lilies from the acorn?
I too dislike it: there are things that are important beyond all this fiddle.

Resign them, sign them, seal them, send them, motion them with breath.
I told you it was easy! . . . Words are fools.
(Boots—boots—boots—boots, moving up an' down again!)

And as things have been they remain.
My little horse must think it queer.

MARTIN McGOWAN

Wet Bones

Let us begin and carry up this corpse.
The armless ambidextrian was lighting
A bracelet of bright haire about the bone.
The bitch bit off his arms at the elbows.

The rattle of the bones, and chuckle spread from ear to ear,
And many a skeleton shook his hand.

I placed a jar in Tennessee
Among the pickled fetuses and bottled bones.
Full many a gem of purest ray serene
Rise from black sea: great dark bulks of hot blood.

Great lovers lie in Hell, the stubborn ones
Picked his bones in whispers. As he rose and fell
The dice of drowned men's bones he saw bequeath
The liquefaction of her clothes.
"I am sleepy, and the oozy weeds about me twist."

By the waters of Babylon we sat down and wept
That such stout fellows left their bones behind.
... But I *was* dead, an hour or more.
I shook the softening chalk of my bones.

"Grill me some bones," said the Cobbler.
The typist home at tea time, clears her breakfast, lights
Bones white with a thousand frosts.

War's dust-bin chariot drawing near,
My marrow beat as wildly as my pulse.
I who am dead a thousand years,
Of his bones are Corrall made.

SUSAN McLEAN

Last Words: A Cento

For certain years, for certain months and days,
I measure time by how a body sways.
Everything we look upon is blest;
only we die in earnest—that's no jest.

When sleep comes down to seal the weary eyes
and gathering swallows twitter in the skies,
rage, rage against the dying of the light,
but keep that earlier, wilder image bright.

We shall go mad no doubt and die that way,
with the slow smokeless burning of decay,
the grass below—above the vaulted sky.
Last of all last words spoken is goodbye.

MARY MOORE

Emily, Walking

I started Early—Took my Dog—
And went against the World—
I had no Cause to be awake—
Creator—Was it you?

A Murmur in the Trees—to note—
And in the Handsome Skies
The Motions of the Dipping Birds—
A pleading Pageantry—

A chilly Peace infests the Grass
Of which it is the sign—
The things we thought that we should do
Make Life a sudden price.

This Me - that walks and works—must die,
The great exchange of clime—
A darting fear—a pomp—a tear—
And the Surrender—Mine—

MARY MOORE

View from a Hotel in Conshohocken, Pennsylvania

In my room, the world is beyond my understanding;
It is the window that makes it difficult
To stop the whirlwind, balk the elements.

Poetry is a finikin thing of air
Singing, with smaller and still smaller sound,
Is a cloud in which a voice mumbles.

The poet mumbles and the painter sees,
But muted, mused, and perfectly revolved
Since what we think is never what we see.

The plainness of plain things is savagery,
In a repetitiousness of men and flies.
Pipperoo, pippera, pipperum . . . The rest is rot.

Widen your sense. All things in the sun are sun.
Was the sun concoct for angels or for men?
How high that highest candle lights the dark.

A blue pigeon it is, that circles the blue sky,
Among the choirs of wind and wet and wing.
And I taste at the root of the tongue the unreal of what is real.

WILDA MORRIS

Astrophel and Stella

—a cento-sonnet

Gone is the winter of my misery!
Her grant to me by her own virtue know;
My thought I speak, and what I speak doth flow
Made manifest by such a victory.
My tongue doth itch, my thoughts in labour be:
The baiting place of wit, the balm of woe,
I now have learned Love right, and learned even so
Where truth itself must speak like flattery.
Stella, food of my thoughts, heart of my heart;
No force, no fraud, robbed they of they delight,
And love doth hold my hand and make me write.
Thou art my Wit, and thou my Virtue art.
While Love on me doth all his quiver spend
My wit doth strive those passions to defend.

CHIRSTOPHER MULROONEY

cento

what gift to match thy god-given hour of happiness
a flower born within a garden close
unknown of cattle uncut of plow
gentled by the air sun-hardened raised by rain
the many boys and many girls long after

Catullus gives you greatmost thanks
and he the worst of poets ranks
so much the worst of poets ranks
as you the bestmost of all patrons

leave off every thought of any reward
nor ever hope to see a man that's grateful

EILEEN MURPHY

when it rains   (*Clouds* Cento #5)

when it rains

how sweet it is to snuggle down and snore away
         let your thinking loose—with thread around its foot

                frogs from pomegranate peel, fleas' footprints
                quivering poplar leaves

                they're laughing as plane trees whisper softly to the elms

(it may well be) you move on to physical desires

a honey cake outside your wool blankets

                the one there with long hair, the spinner of words
                wearing a yellow tunic and over that a lion skin

EILEEN MURPHY

Grimm Cento #2

      How dark it was inside
whirring and crowding.

You have no clothes   godless witch,

I will eat

                                    her foot.

                Open the stomach

and cut   a bit off her.

          Do I find you here,

      to be smeared and   slipped

and her mother stood by   like a squirrel.

Ha, I am glad that no one   belonged. She escaped

so deep into the   stunted kitchen

                    and said mockingly,

O you fool,
                    Turn and peep, turn and peep
and saw how
                    the blood
                              has
shut the door
covered with cakes   and   built of bread

            until the festival
            began with pitch

                        an axe stuck

and   she devoured   the   shoe.

ERIC NELSON

Dickinson's Island

Because I could not stop for death—
He kindly stopped for me.
So sit right back and you'll hear a tale,
A tale of a fateful trip.

We slowly drove—He knew no haste,
The skipper brave and sure.
We passed the fields of gazing grain
For a three hour tour.

No phones, no lights, no motor cars
Not a single luxury,
The carriage held but just ourselves
And Immortality.

The weather started getting rough,
A swelling of the Ground.
The Dews drew quivering and chill—
Only gossamer my gown.

Since then—'tis Centuries—and yet
Feels shorter than the Day
That started from a tropic port
Aboard this tiny ship.

DEBORAH NODLER ROSEN

Dreaming Myself

Waiting for darkness and a place to shine—
Darkness restores what light cannot repair,
Stalks the perimeter of an enormous dream.
We dream our way back—
Home's the place we head for in our sleep.

My life, this shirt I want to take off.
Why do I long to be devoured and to forget in life rather than in death
The ancient war between obsession and responsibility?

Today is always gone tomorrow; Nowhere is all around us.
The cries of those who vanish might take years to get here
For entrance can never be the same as exit.
Don't waste your time with recollection or prophecy,
Our hands want to plant something that will bloom tomorrow.

Our deep human labor to become spirits;
Our almost vegetal need to be reborn.
All with our feet bound stiff in the skins of the conquered.
I have had it all and want it back again—
Time in its transparent loops as it passes beneath me now.

The fear of death is as ubiquitous as light. It illuminates everything.
Trembling in anticipation of first petal-fall, announcement of death's commencement,
Which leaves us finally tattooed and senseless trembling on the stair,
For it was, we eventually came to see, the sound of our own perishing.
Like what we imagine knowledge to be: dark, salt, clear, moving, utterly free.

It is not the fire we hunger for and not the ash,
It is the still hour.
I crave those voices dreaming in my sleep.

GEORGE NORTHRUP

Nos Morituri Te Salutamus

We who are about to—
being of sound mind and seeking
to arrange our worldly affairs
in anticipation of that end which awaits all men
We who tremble naked in this
tall and decent light
were not indifferent sport
in yesterday's arena.
setting aside all prior bequests
We who, as you have, Titus,
enjoyed the spectacle,
but from the other side—
We who are about to
know the lion's kiss—
leave all our worldly possessions
We who are about to
march behind these final words
into the mouth of silence
now
salute you.

KATHLEEN OSSIP

Ballade Confessionnelle: Plath and Sexton

They're out of the dark's ragbag, these two—
two cramped girls breathing carelessly.
No day is safe from news of you,
though the oarlocks stick and are rusty,
heavy and rigid in a pool of glue.
The night nurse is passing.
The world is full of enemies.
I couldn't stop looking.

They tell you to go, and you do
with the help of the red-haired secretary.
You say your husband is just no good to you.
That's what it means to be crazy.
The permanent guests have done nothing new.
I confess I am only broken by the sources of things:
a pane of dragonfly wing, when they left me.
I couldn't stop looking.

The skulls, the unbuckled bones facing the view!
In a dream, you are never eighty.
They're the real thing, all right: the Good, the True
that glide ahead of the very thirsty
and the locked drops rising in a dew.
The cup of coffee is growing and growing.
So much for psychology.
I couldn't stop looking.

Fading out like an old movie,
it was not a heart, beating.
I love them like history.
I couldn't stop looking.

LYNNE PATTISON

Who But I

Admit me to your story
Irregular and passionate

Admit me to your possible
Your cold shiver eyes

Wells of uncanny
light—a door

Who but I
In this cold light rushed

The nude sky to risk
Your deafening thunder

All the mild days—rain
A cold shiver—travelers bypass this door

I come kicking errors and lies
Down the green streets

Considering rumours
Of drowned voices—voyeur angels

To learn sudden order
bred of sweet silences

bone tight cold—the wish
of sand parch

For the sweet stretch
and warm arch of lawn

DAVID POSTON

Cento, Selected Works

"Change," they said, sea talk from an old book of riddles,
bedlam et cetera.
                    Listen with the eye,
taste and remember what the light was like.
           Six kinds of creature—
cloud sun fountain statue teeth and bones.
Twelve moons, a stun of jewels, bright November,
every star a tongue, water breathing air.
Tongue without hands,
the bread god whispering to fool the wind.

Put thou thy tears into my bottle.
To fuck is to love again; *kyrie eleison kerista.*
Blessings, the body gave, bread rather than blossoms.
              The love bit,
the natural need, baptism of desire,
                the moods of love.
Sunday is a day of incest, my daughters, my sisters.
You come singing tunes for bears to dance to.
Picnic, lightning, words to the wind.

Beware, soul brother, Christmas in Biafra,
        Moscow in the wilderness, Segovia in the snow,
                night shift at the crucifix factory,
the death bell once for the last bandit,
the dream of Jake Hopkins,
the nightmare factory, a shot in the park.

Why is the house dissolving? To see the matter clearly,
archaeology is a destructive science. The terrible shears the world.
I breathe the sorrows of cold stone to the place of trumpets.
Figments of the firmament, where water comes together with other water.
Pictures of the gone world,
the work of one night in the dark, solitary confinement,
New Jersey State Prison, Trenton.
        From the avenue bearing the initial of Christ into the new world,
John nobody, walking underwater, leaves
and ashes the color as,
naked, the darkness surrounds us,
the color of dust.

        High tide in the garden,
the garden where all loves end.
After every green thing forty days, apple nights, the dark flags of waking.
The girl in the yellow raincoat, walking past midnight, walking to sleep,
her body against time, black shawl moon in a mason jar.
Angel, interrupted, this close to the earth.
Color is the suffering of light gathering the mountains,
the stone harp, freedom's plow.
Beyond the withered oak ten thousand saplings grow
poem rising out of the earth and standing up in someone.
Praise
to the end
       some things
words can do.

MARJORIE POWER

Fall Runway Report

If you could pack only two cosmetics,
remember: beautiful clothes don't
always have to have a rosy outlook.
The most important silhouette this season
delves deep into the tenacity of the human spirit,
which mournful music always fills me with
a dramatic counterpoint to beige lips.
His cocky intellect is, in a sense,
the main character, thrusting its way
past the pitfalls of feelings, stopping
at the precipice of a nervous breakdown.
To suit every archetype, the style
is offered in two sizes and three colors.

MARJORIE POWER

Wander Woman

I tell Gabriel it's time to get back on the road.
So we trespass. We drive that private road
right to its end. Traditional squirrel stew
on an open fire. If it's cooked, eat it. Why not,
indeed. The highlights of the trip are always incidental.
An intense, even savage attention to life's fine print.
Bluegrass and moonshine. The main in the chair
spits shave lather into the air. It swirls through
smoky restaurants and darkening courtyards.
This fall, the mummies will be shown.
The mummies feel like family to many people.
The decision to push on despite being lost.
You won't find these tips in any guide book.
Avoid poring over a large map in public. Stay
vigilant. Watch your wallet. Most importantly, move on.

ANN PRIVATEER

Dove Promises

Smile, people will wonder
what you've been up to,

savor every happy moment,
laugh uncontrollably . . .

it clears the mind, wink at someone
driving past. Today, life, joy,

chocolate. Sing along
with the elevator music,

don't think about it so much,
be fearless. You know what?

You look good in red.

ANN PRIVATEER

Untitled

An untitled, unsigned, self-portrait
of Van Gogh's Sunflowers in a Rose
Arbor depict Mt. Fuji on a Clear Day.

Me and the Moon sit Near an Open
Window, nude. The Kiss, A Seated
Woman With Bent Knee rests her head

near The Old Poorhouse dead, A Woman
with a Glass Bottle, The Cheat With The ace
of Diamonds, Doubting Thomas,

The Wreck of Hope, Little Yellow Horses
Surrounded by Scenes of His Life Resurrected
With Christ and The Madonna With the Long Neck.

Two Venetian Ladies Cross the Street
Near the San Lorenzo Bridge. Three Ages
of Man and Death. The Unreal City.

A Portrait of a Degenerate Artist,
Red Stone Dancer, Girl With White Dog,
A Giant Hamburger, and The Chocolate Pot . . .

BURT RASHBAUM

Stolen Wind Poem

I sometimes sleep
and wonder what's wrong.
Wind is a survival mechanism.
The wind.
The bigger the body. . . .
Something is afoot.

It makes me edgy,
pushes me ahead.
The influences of pain
are blown in by hot, dry
wind.

The winter emotions:
profound distress.
It can't calm down (open your car doors).

Sleep patterns
and particularly gusty locales
bow from the wind.
I learned this.

Uses for wind:
wind sites,
excellent wind
(defined as excellent),
the location
just downwind of

an entire windy country,
erratic and strong.

In the eastern provinces.
From all directions.
People from town
With the "for sale" signs
go right.

STEVEN REIGNS

To My Ex

I can taste you're still alive.
You were wild, where are you now?
You know me so well.

I guess what I'm seeking isn't here.
Seems I keep getting the story twisted,
cutting my hands up every time I touch you.

I know you've seen fire.
The spire is hot and
I don't need much to keep me warm.
Will you hold me for just a fair time?

God knows, I've thrown away those graces.
I can't claim innocence,
I know I've been driven like the snow.

I get a little warm in my heart
'cause even the sun's got a price on it.
I don't think you even know.
Hold back a glacier,
somethings are melting now.
Can't forget the things you never said.
Snow can wait,
I forgot my mittens.

ALICITA RODRÍGUEZ

Map of Bones

There was a grand feast
as if time were made for nourishment alone.
A delicious perfume came
pompous with treasures.

A rattle of plates and dishes
exquisite as chimes—
and under the tongues
a history of flutes.

The cauldron simmers
with dragon's blood, to coat the body.
Fancy it on the table:
bowl of blue shade.

And sip the cold sweet wine
in a small glass,
an ornament
glittering and sparkling all lovely colours.

Sweeping abundance overtaking
its apples so red, and its grapes so blue;
sky's blue vault
for a phalanx of grapefruit trees.

Sit down and toy with my mouth
and let go, tongue's soft release
rejoicing as if stained
soft translucent peach.

We are all finishing
the sweet erotic pulp—
certainly less sweet
the banquet done.

ALICITA RODRÍGUEZ

Lion Tamarins

With rising, triumphant ardor,
        the whole of the golden mass
                slipped by the terrace, made a sudden leap—

to inhabit the air.

Above the forest of the parakeets,
        from blossom to blossom and always
                hanging innocently

in a sovereign floating of joy.

Bright topaz denizens of a world of green
        vanished in a crepuscular noise,
                and now the night swells with their chitter,

of tiny breathing threads.

LORRAINE SCHEIN

Word Balloon

She has entered a liminal state.
Cloud-hair.
Thought bubbles
The Invisible Woman.
Comics, like a recurrent childhood dream . . .
Asgard has fallen onto New York.
Narnia will, too.
Doop's brain is about to explode.
Too weird to be a member of the mutants.
Ability to hear unvoiced thoughts.
Psionic being, attempting a chaos hex—
Your reality is now being repaired.
Penciler, Pym Particles.
Supersentient being.
Janus, the Nega-Man.
The Negative Zone.
Tail error.
Concussive Optic Blasts.
The universe is a dream that dreams.
Who is the mysterious power princess?
. . . Abandoned surface life for a time.
My kingdom is a lonely one,
where the occult and the everyday intermingle,
where the superhuman and the supernatural meet . . .
Water will conquer air, Airlings!

NANCY SCOTT

Now Is the Time

>—after an ink drawing, *Ya es tiempo*,
>by Aramis Gutierrez

I.

History counts its skeletons in round numbers
Those who lead the country into the abyss

Leaders of armies, big capitalists, great executioners

They lie, bribe, dance on the dead bodies

With the wolves of the marketplace

II.

Now is the time

        Our fever's menacing shapes are precise and alive

        A half-witted woman with loose hair is weeping
        She is weeping for her lost right arm

        She runs out into the moonlight and its horror

                the haystacks and houses are burning
                the hills are scorched black
                moon like cold stone

Now is the time

        We are left alone . . . and the time is short
        Wild wolves have broken through the gates

WENDY SHORTRIDGE

Blood Bath

The ways of war slay me, the pity of war.

Jabbed and killed, the groans and piteous cries

of dying men. Twisted limbs, bloody clothes,

distressful hands grasping for hands grown

loath and cold. Universal cries for Mother

crescendos from all decaying lips.

Titanic wars devour as nations trek from progress,

dull granite tombs enshrine the honored dead.

Vain citadels to political standoffs,

invasions of the spirit without stint.

I knew you in this dark, strange friend,

I knew we stood in Hell.

We sacrificed the wildest beauty in the world

for graying, senile sycophants.

LUCILLE GANG SHULKLAPPER

Fury

    —for Mama

My mother never forgave my father
She sits at the foot of the bed.
Each lonely and earthly, wanting to be celestial.

I went to them. And now I know
Who hears the rain churning the forest to mud,
Who had no guide, no stone,
Where the bedclothes lie in stagnant coils on the bed.

From you I want more than I've ever asked,
In those years, people will say, we lost track.
What was this world? Where things you never did
have come in their slow way into
An agitation of the air.

Age may come, parting may come, death will come.
Parents don't want to face the children's rage,
I will you to see her as she was, to ride
all the bright clouds and clusters,
Of her hidden life
A woman cornered, a plaintive shadow.

MARTHA SILANO

New Mother Cento

1.
Having choices is a blessing.
How and when do I introduce them?
A minimum of four times a day.
Is this normal? More study is needed.

2.
A cushion of three to six months.
A whole new world of hazards.
It's so easy! Have an expert check
your genitals, so she doesn't catch a cold.

3.
If you find yourself breathing too heavily,
gently press the buttock cheeks, pinching
the skin, or "shush" near her ear.
It may even spark your latent exhibitionism!

4.
There's no evidence that you should make drastic changes,
even if he doesn't do everything the way you would.
We won't want to make life so miserable.
Just fifteen minutes a day strengths hamstrings and calves.

5.
We don't want to frighten, but don't be surprised
if you need a lubricant. Pick your best feature
and accentuate. Soft music. Shooting pain.
Cuddle . . . her belly tight again your own.

TOREY SIMONS

Trichechus manatus latirostris

Between the ocean and the sky. You might see clearly,
In the carnal sun, clothed in a hymn of flies,
a tossing, vertiginous colonnade of foam, up above—

a sacred place
Delicacy of warm Florida waters,

and colors and sizes coming out of our woods
we sigh and slide ourselves down from the benches
plunging down, flattening
in the slippery wet, a hollow space,

we go to sea
in our explorations, we come face to face
Harmless together.

DANNY SKLAR

Never Start a Sentence with *There*

There is no remedy for love
but to love more.
There is in my nature, methinks,
a singular yearning toward wildness.
"There are two asleep in the cave,"
the gypsy said.
There has been a kind of confusion
in my conscousness.
There is no clear light, no clear shadow
in remembering.
There are two ways of spreading light:
to be the candle
or the mirror that reflects it.
There is no better day than
today to see God.
There was a child went forth every day.
There is that in me—I don't know what it is—
but I know it is in me.
There in the room as I wake from sleep
this vision presses upon me.
There is the camp, one regement
departs tomorrow.
There in the crowd stood I and singled
you out with attachment.
There we two, content, happy in being
together, speaking little
perhaps not a word.
There in a huge kettle of boiling water

the lobsters shall be boiled till their
color becomes scarlet.
There are many right answers.
There are many ways to see things.
There was a bar adjoining, but nobody
cared about alcohol.
There she was standing in the yard
barefooted, with little barefooted Prajna,
as I walked off along the horse meadow.
There are more things in heaven
and earth, Horatio, than are dreamt
of in your philosophy.
There is a world elsewhere.
There is a world elsewhere.

JEANNE STAUFFER-MERLE

A Cento of Houses

1

Lip up over the steps all night

Invading the distance between soil and words
the little walls break up and bleed
then absence, the open room
a step scattered with straw
and the wheelbarrow jammed
but empty—
indifferent noons leading to the ripple of a question:
And is it as I have become?

I make my corners.
They turn to stones, dark and light stones in a scattered mosaic
retreating backwards until their long lost premises turn inside out—
le jour tomb.

> The day is like wide water, without sound.
> Here there is an ill, flat
> something like a house
> of twilight. Children's shriekings filter and drain.

2

For Whom a Square Room is a Fire

      I could say I am a ferry boat—
            a protracted wait that is also night.
            Round and round goes the bell of water.

      Now I could scatter my body.
            Either the white wave has receded
                or on the beaches—

wishes
of rose and ice
an indigence of light.

3

Of Soft, Dizzying Light.

O distinct
pale, pale blue distance—
you have taken the summer house, the hedge—
do you remember how we used to gather?
Were you trying to talk to me last night?

You draw the black straw out of me.
But you forget everything.

BARBARA TAYLOR

On *Silk and Soul*

—*a dedication to Dr Nina Simone*

Ooh child, cherish is a word—
tell it like it is to be young gifted and black,
in the morning to love somebody,
in the dark the backlash blues.
Do I move you?
I can't see nobody,
I wish I knew how it would
feel to be free.

Wild is the wind,

you turn me on. Where can I go

without you?

Here comes the sun, The High Priestess of Soul.

Turning Point, I get along without you

very well.

Where is the human touch? Isn't

it a pity, Mississippi goddam,

everyone's gone to the moon.

Another Spring, since I fell for you,

seems I'm never tired

loving you. Please, don't let

me be misunderstood

ne me quitte pas, I ain't got no, I got life.

Please read me

I want a little sugar in my bowl,

peace and joy divine, forever.

Your final consummation:

take my hand precious Lord,

do what you gotta do,

I think it's going to rain today.

BARBARA TAYLOR

Things to Remember

A Robin Redbreast in a cage
 puts all heaven in a rage.
He who shall hurt the little wren
 shall never be beloved by men.
Lying is done with words
 and also with silence.
Truth does not change
 according to our ability
to stomach it. Every
 creature is better alive
than dead, men and moose
 and pine trees, and he who
understands it aright will
 rather preserve its life than
destroy it—it is forbidden
 to kill; therefore all murderers
are punished unless they kill
 in large numbers and to the
sound of trumpets!!! Now I see
 the secret of the making of
the best persons. It is to grow
 in the open air and to eat
and sleep with the earth.
 When the power of love
overcomes the love
 of power the world
will know peace.

JUANITA TORRENCE-THOMPSON

A Cento of Lucy Angeleri's Poetry

Unborn, free
streams of
cognizance

I am desperate for a place of my own

I curl into this mind
scene and start to feel the soft water
lapping my feet:

some day
I will fall
into pockets of mass

. . . walk
through the facade
sprayed with lemon sun

A cloud-burst will inundate

hymns and sweet verbiage
  . . . chanting

Finally, a moment
of grace   and blessed silence

CATHERINE TUFARIELLO

Spamtoum

For Camshaft Cohen, Earline Gee,
Cook Bullocks, Busby Salazar,
Spigot P. Toxicity
and others who know who they are.

The Last Wish of a Dying Man
Get an iPod nano Free!
Cheap Viagra. Tryptophan.
Why are you ignoring me?

Get an iPod nano Free!
Do you wish for lager Breast?
Why are you ignoring me?
I need to get this off my chest

Do you wish for lager Breast?
They're beautiful looking rich chiffon
I need to get this off my chest
Urgent message from Amazon

They're beautiful looking rich chiffon
This could be your lucy day!
Urgent message from Amazon
Cut your bills the Christian way

This could be your lucy day!
This thing here could change your life
Cut your bills the Christian way
Hide cable watching from your Wife

This thing here could change your life
Trojans everywhere slay them all
Hide cable watching from your Wife
ha ha your penis is so small

Trojans everywhere slay them all
My sylvan swim go private snog
ha ha your penis is so small
you fat ass stochastic frog

my sylvan swim go private snog
"You've Been Sent an Insta-Kiss!"
you fat ass stochastic frog
Get rid of messages like this

"You've Been Sent an Insta-Kiss!"
Cheap Viagra. Tryptophan.
Get rid of messages like this
The Last Wish of a Dying Man

HELEN TZAGOLOFF

Cento

Walking homeward I fraternize with shadows
swoop in a flock across grass, see a stranger cry
among speechless women beating their little ones.

The star laughs from its rotting shroud
on the old shore, lit by the moon.
It won't shift an inch. It won't ache to touch.

The silence unmoving, plunging past gravity,
tipped back in the cup of my hand,
boredom a poison with no antidote.

There's an old ache in my brain
curled and tightened.
What are we in the hands of the great God?

Our needs are sores upon our nakedness
waltzing together on pale tumbled blooms.
Yet in my clumsiness I found a place.

I ride on my own diminishing. I grow gray,
adequate for survival, withstanding all knocks.
Luck is something I do not understand.

HELEN TZAGOLOFF

Midnight

Bride of the lion walking after midnight
Through a dark mist, moonlight magic
Sweet tomorrows, wildest heart

Stand-in husband, midnight masquerade
Where shadows go wild, twilight whispers
Her secret, his child, bittersweet bygones

Wild Jasmine under the desert moon
A dark rider, midnight raider
Prince of dreams, morning comes softly

Wolf in waiting, pure sin beyond scandal
Rose without a thorn moonfire
Dove at midnight chanting surrender

Sunset embrace, fulfillment unconquered
Till dawn tames the night, almost Eden
November of the heart midnight secrets

PATRICIA VALDATA

Cento: The Waves Are Running in Verses

The world is a mist. And then the world is
Cold dark deep and absolutely clear
Suddenly turning dangerous.

Here is a coast; here is a harbor;
Turning to waterfalls under our very eyes.
The waves are running in verses this fine morning.

Wasted, wasted minutes that couldn't be worse,
Whatever the landscape had of meaning appears to have been abandoned
In watery prismatic white-and-blue.

With these the monotonous, endless, sagging coast-line,
Plus all that vulgar beauty of iridescence,
Sinks through the drift of bodies,

Lifting them fringed with heavy drops,
Drifting simultaneously to the same height,
Wet, stuck, purple, among the dead-eye pearls.

SUSAN VOLCHOK

Standing Here/Now

—In honor of the publication of False Horizon, *by Sue Standing*

I

This poem remembers the summer
created topographies of doubt:
past the monastery and up to
the country of desire
full of pink-snouted spotted pigs and overflowing corncribs.
The square square miles. Water rising.
That must have been then,
hammered together by an inept carpenter:
Unsay it. Gainsay it.
A perfume made of coal and tar.
An exhausted wash of cloud
is otherwise. A darkening mirror
which once held the beauty and sorrows of women.
Love stretched thinner than a wishbone.
Everything in the rain.

II

She hoped their love would not prove fugitive,
a knifethrower's kiss on the template of the body.
But whose naked narrative will suffice?
Choose: backward or forward.
Who are you anyway?
The good life breezes by the grafted trees.
Things happen in time,
the crosswalk signal says.
I want a house-shaped house
that you might come to love,
might keep you,
a room, a table, paper and pencil.
Above this latitude of lassitude,
past pink thistles on which bees impale themselves:
How did you learn to leave him?
The echo of loon calls,
of musical hysteria.
Grief is endless and invisible.
No bones, only flesh and restlessness.
But yesterday in the buoyant waters
Your thighs of igneous rock
the cascade's inside me—

III

Skin is skin when your own limbs are electric.
Impossible to keep anything. Impossible,
impossible to translate.
Perhaps she has lost herself in loss.
After was after all.
It's lonely here, without a doubt,
a room inside a room inside a room—
they call it continuity.
All night, you can hear the loud *beep beep beep*
in the style of Fellini, not Truffaut—
did you know that *irrisou*,
that bits of language like potsherds,
like the prizes at the peche *aux canards*, set
voices rising from under the lindens:
soyez prudent.
I make my call and walk back through
impatiens and petunias,
and into the oak woods where the path divides.
Why don't places remember people?

IRVING WEISS

Team Poem

Appease this virtuous enemy of man
The way which thou so well hast learn'd below,
And dwell, as in my center as I can,
As into air the purer spirits flow—
Thou whose exterior semblance doth belie
A chronicle of actions just & bright,
Cheerful & fresh as ever: let us try
The grave of joy, prison of day's delight.
Whom thousand souls devoutly idolize
Full in the smile of the blue firmament,
Rise in thy heart & gather to the eyes
With glist'ring beams, gold streaming where they bent.
      To sing again, beneath the shadowy trees,
        Of tempests can no more disturb thy ease.

THERESA MALPHRUS WELFORD

Fatima

It's terrible to be a woman in this world.
A woman's reputation is her soul. It's her heart and gizzard.
You let them rape and murder you
before you let them do anything to your reputation.

Am I believing my ears?
What do you know about anything?
What are you saying
about my country, my heart and soul?

I am sixteen. I am returned to die again, again, again.
The Israelis come for me. A foolish girl. I was left in a room somewhere,
and I waited. Such waiting is worse than a beating.
Worse than death. I've been waiting to go out. I am waiting.

After four days alone with misery,
I am let go of their prison,
I am left even by enemies.
And they let me live.

What of my parents' shame, driven off the good land
and sacred home the father's fathers built? When we were homeless
and dying without food, what of the four starving babies
I had to bury still alive, living? I, I, I?

Ten months, ten years, ten centuries! What of my losses?
My punishment, at the hands of God,
for all the food those babies would eaten.
Can I buy a bar of American soap and wash these away?

You have to *make* children see.
This the first time I say it out loud.
I think, maybe if I don't say it,
maybe, does it go away.

But it don't. It comes, it comes, it comes.
I knew it! I knew it! *Here* there no escape!
Don't do this to me.
Listen to that! Do you hear?

THERESA MALPHRUS WELFORD

Like a Wide River

—for Mark

Here is the deepest secret nobody knows:
My love has two lives, in order to love you:
That's why I love you when I do not love you,
And also why I love you when I do.
I stand with you braced against the wind.

Close your dreams, Love, enter my eyes with your skies,
Spread out through my blood like a wide river.
I don't know who it is who lives or dies, who rests or wakes,
But it is your heart that distributes
All the graces of the daybreak, in my breast.

I carry you with me everywhere.
And now you're mine. Rest with your dream in my dream.
We will go together, over the waters of time.
No one else will travel through the shadows with me,
Only you, evergreen, ever sun, ever moon.

I feel I've always been here; that, even then,
Years ago, until I understood, Love:
I was standing where I stand now,
Emptied of longing, waiting for you,
my dark familiar clay.

My life, which I gave to you, fills
With years like a swelling cluster of fruit.
When I die, I want your hands on my eyes:
I want what I love to continue to live:
I shall but love thee better after death.

I could kneel and praise all small forgotten miracles,
my place, a land of kisses and volcanoes,
a landscape short of rain, bare against the sky,
my heart's future: It is poured out like water,
it is melted like wax.

INGRID WENDT

Paraphrase in Time of Thaw

—A collage for William Stafford

And what does the river say, agelessly
pulsing along, awake
to its own part of forever,
to all multiple ways of belonging, gathering

traces of ridge top, wind litanies
creasing the thin skins of glaciers, those millions of
crow's feet trickling down and away, gathering
sunlight, its party the rain; gathering

certainty: all is
attached, in constant revision. Tight fists
of boulders unfolding. Like lines in the palm,
like fortunes weathered away, converging at sea.

And again in the air. What
the river says, the birds repeat.
Far from any human allegiance to grudges and
righteousness, their voices proclaim the stars.

And the stars keep passing along what the mountains
rumble: a center the soul can recognize. As in a whirlwind.
That one chosen place buried
somewhere near the lift of an eyebrow, near faith.

What the river says, calls us
to attention, to carrying on.
Someday, maybe, our stumbling echoes
holding one shifting line true.

BIOGRAPHICAL NOTE

Theresa Malphrus Welford, who hails from a working-class background in the state of Georgia, has taught at the University of Georgia, Louisiana State University, Western Carolina University, and the University of Cincinnati. At Georgia Southern, where she currently teaches, she has developed a number of writing courses, including Writing the Animal and Writing the Undead. The students in Theresa's First-Year Writing and Creative Writing courses regularly participate in Books of Hope, in which they research, write, and illustrate books for young readers in Uganda, Africa. Theresa and her husband, who volunteer with local animal-rescue groups, are the happy parents of ten animals, former rescues all.

Theresa is currently working on several projects: creative nonfiction, poetry, and storybooks for children. She has published poetry, essays, articles, and book chapters, as well as *The Paradelle: An Anthology* (Red Hen Press, 2005). Her book *Trans-Atlantic Connections: The Movement and New Formalism* is forthcoming from Story Line Press.